Answered Prayer

*A True Story of a Woman's Personal Struggle
for a Deeper Walk with God and How
He Answered Her Deepest Prayer*

Josie Blocher

WestBow
PRESS
A DIVISION OF THOMAS NELSON

Copyright © 2013 Josie Blocher.

*Artwork by C. Michael Dudash "He Shall Hear My Voice"
Somerset Fine Art—Michael Dudash Prints and Canvas available at
www.SomersetFineArt.com*

*All rights reserved. No part of this book may be used or reproduced by any means,
graphic, electronic, or mechanical, including photocopying, recording, taping or by any
information storage retrieval system without the written permission of the publisher
except in the case of brief quotations embodied in critical articles and reviews.*

WestBow Press books may be ordered through booksellers or by contacting:

*WestBow Press
A Division of Thomas Nelson
1663 Liberty Drive
Bloomington, IN 47403
www.westbowpress.com
1-(866) 928-1240*

*Because of the dynamic nature of the Internet, any web addresses or links contained in
this book may have changed since publication and may no longer be valid. The views
expressed in this work are solely those of the author and do not necessarily reflect the
views of the publisher, and the publisher hereby disclaims any responsibility for them.*

*Any people depicted in stock imagery provided by Thinkstock are models,
and such images are being used for illustrative purposes only.*

Certain stock imagery © Thinkstock.

*ISBN: 978-1-4908-0085-1 (sc)
ISBN: 978-1-4908-0087-5 (hc)
ISBN: 978-1-4908-0086-8 (e)*

Library of Congress Control Number: 2013912248

Printed in the United States of America.

WestBow Press rev. date: 7/10/2013

Dedicated to:

Him that is able to do exceeding abundantly above all that we ask or think

Ephesians 3:20

My Prayer

Dear Lord,
I come before thee as a child comes to a parent,
Knowing that you can fix everything, and you love me.
I also know that you will only do me good
All the days of my life.
I come before you trusting, knowing that you
"Know those who trust in thee."
I believe that "every detail," no matter how small,
Is ordained by thy loving hand.
I know you will never leave me nor forsake me.
I love you Lord. It is you, who gives me strength,
Protects me, and comforts me.
You know my every worry. You know my deepest pain.
You know my secret faults, and my secret sins.
You are the only one I need. I need no other.
Thank you for your never failing love,
And thank you Lord for hearing me
While I'm on my knees in prayer.

Amen

When what I know
In my heart and mind
Goes deeper than my pain.
'Tis then I know
The love of God
Transcends through all the same.

Contents

Prologue xi

Chapter 1: Through the Eyes of a Child 1
Chapter 2: The Day I Got Saved 9
Chapter 3: Summer Of Sorrow 13
Chapter 4: Life without Daddy 19
Chapter 5: A Friend 25
Chapter 6: Life-Changing Decisions 33
Chapter 7: Worldly Influences 39
Chapter 8: College Days 45
Chapter 9: A New Beginning 51
Chapter 10: Our First Year 57
Chapter 11: Married Life 61
Chapter 12: A Church Family 65
Chapter 13: My Darkest Days 73
Chapter 14: Renewal 81
Chapter 15: The Farm House 85
Chapter 16: The Five-Acre Farm 97
Chapter 17: Growing in Grace 113
Chapter 18: Following His Lead 123
Chapter 19: Starting Anew 127
Chapter 20: Tragedy 131
Chapter 21: Reflections 139

About the Author 153

Prologue

*The eyes of the Lord are over the righteous,
and his ears are open unto their prayers.*

1 Peter 3:12

It was the summer of 1958. I was nine years old, and my family consisted of Daddy, Mother, Margaret, Walter, and me. We were in Vancouver, British Columbia, Canada, on one of Daddy's evangelistic trips. He was to be the guest speaker at a Christian family Bible camp. He was driving our loaded-down Hudson, which we kids called the flying banana, through the mountains. It was an extremely hot July day, and the heat seemed to penetrate to the bone.

The mountain road seemed like one continuous curve on a steady incline. On our left side was a drop-off straight down, which seemed to go down for miles, and on our right side was a wall of rocks straight up. We hadn't seen another car for hours. We three kids sat in the back seat and Mother and Daddy were in the front seat.

Daddy was ill from the heat. Several years earlier Daddy had suffered a heat stroke while in the Mojave Desert on one of our other evangelistic trips to California. Now, this extreme heat had made him ill again.

Daddy was not the only one with problems. Our old Hudson wasn't running right. The car was going slower and slower until finally it stalled on the steep mountain slope. Daddy put on the emergency brakes, but slowly they started to slip.

Weary, and almost ready to faint, Daddy pulled out his white handkerchief and hung it on the radio antenna, and then he told us all to pray. Boy did I pray! I even turned around in the back seat and prayed on my knees leaning on the seat. I was scared to death. We all prayed for God's help and intervention. "Call upon me in the day of trouble: I will deliver thee, and thou shalt glorify me" (Psalm 50:15).

Suddenly, out of nowhere, a car came around the curve of the mountain. The driver saw we were in distress, and the car stopped. Out stepped a young man. He asked us if we needed help. Would you believe, he was a mechanic and just so happened to have all the tools needed to fix our car. Isn't God wonderful! After repairing our car, the young man drove on his way. Daddy was still suffering from the heat, but he resumed driving the car up the steep mountain road to the Bible camp. We never saw another car. I truly believe that God sent an angel that day. "Be not forgetful to entertain strangers: for thereby some have entertained angels unawares" (Hebrews 13:2). Such was the type of faith I was raised on.

> While there is life there is hope and while
> there is hope there is room for prayer.
> —Matthew Henry

Chapter 1

Through the Eyes of a Child

Thy faithfulness is unto all generations . . .

Psalm 119:90

I was born in Roseau, Minnesota, on March 29, 1949. I was the youngest in the family and the only one born in the United States. My father, Reverend Marzelius Hausmann, known as Mark Houseman, was born in 1908, in Minsk, Russia (in a region known as White Russia), before the Russian Revolution of 1917. He escaped to the United States and became an ordained Baptist minister and evangelist. He wrote his autobiography, called *Under the Red Star*. My mother, Isobel (Hurlburt) Houseman, was born in Vancouver, British Columbia, Canada, in 1921. The two met at Prairie Bible Institute in the town of Three Hills, Alberta, Canada. Mother was thirteen years younger than Daddy. My sister, Margaret, who we called Margie, was born in Rose Valley, Saskatchewan, Canada, in 1944. My brother, Walter, who we called Wally but who now wants to be called Walt, was born in Wadena, Saskatchewan, in 1945.

Since I was the baby of the family, I was Daddy's favorite, and I was spoiled rotten. I'd scream and holler, causing Daddy to come running, and I'd say, "Wally did it." And while Wally was being spanked, I'd smile at him mischievously. He'd stare back at me as if saying, "I'm going to kill you." Poor Wally got a lot of spankings he didn't deserve.

But growing up, Wally was my best friend. We did everything together. We would turn the chairs upside down and make a corral. Wally was my horse. I would lead him around with a rope and feed him Cheerios. Margie was five years older than I was, so she thought whatever Wally and I were doing was stupid and childish. She would always sit and read books.

Because Daddy was a pastor, he would go to the jails and preach, and sometimes he took us with him. I remember, as a small girl, standing in front of the men in the jail and singing "Jesus Wants Me for a Sunbeam." All the inmates would say, "Ah, isn't she cute."

Daddy also was an evangelist, so he traveled a lot, and we often went with him. I was in, or at least traveled through, every state in the United States except Hawaii. I remember traveling for hours upon hours. Maybe that's why I don't like traveling today. To entertain myself I would stand behind Daddy and comb his hair. His hair was about two inches long; he always had some type of grease or gel on it, but I didn't mind. I would curl his hair with bobby pins or I would put his hair in little pigtails. Thus, he was driving everywhere looking like an Aunt Jemima doll.

I always got carsick. Mother would let me lie in the front seat between her and Daddy, with my head on her lap, and she would rub my head and belly. I still get carsick to this very day, but I've learned that if I just sit up and look out the window, it will go away.

I was quite the mommy's baby, also. Many times when we stopped at a church where Daddy was the guest preacher, they couldn't accommodate the whole family in one person's home, so they split us up. Mommy and Daddy were in one home, Margie and I were in another home, and Wally was in another home. This was a terrible experience for a mommy's baby. I cried all night long. I can only imagine what I must have put those poor people through. I remember lying in bed, sobbing, repeatedly saying, "I want my mommy."

Margie would say, "For heaven's sake, Josie, I'm your sister."

I'd answer, gasping between each sob and trying to catch my breath, "I don't care. I want Mommy." So it wasn't always good times on our trips.

We resided in many states, each time finding a new house to call our home. Some of the states we lived in were Minnesota, California, Pennsylvania, New Hampshire, and Indiana. In Minnesota, we lived in three homes. The first was in Roseau, Minnesota, where I was born. The next was in International Falls, Minnesota, where Daddy took a pastorate. Then we moved to Minneapolis, Minnesota, for a few months where Daddy was training to be a medic, and then to Chico, California. Mother was already a licensed practical nurse. Daddy and Mother became students at a missionary boot camp under the New Tribes Mission. They were going through training to be missionaries in South America where nurses and medics were needed. But it ended up that they couldn't go because Daddy had a heat stroke.

So we moved to Pennsylvania. I only remember the places we lived by the houses. I don't remember the houses in Minnesota or California, as I was very young when we lived there. However, I do remember the houses in Pennsylvania.

In Pennsylvania we lived in three homes. The first was in Shamokin, Pennsylvania, where I attended kindergarten in a parochial school. It was a mining town. It had lots of hills, and the streets were steep. We lived on a hill in an upstairs apartment. One day I brought home a stray black cat. As soon as I brought him into the house, he threw up worms. There were these long, skinny, spaghetti-like worms rising up and down in a pinkish soup. Mother put her hands in the air, screamed, and yelled, "Get that cat out of this house!" I grabbed him, ran outside, and let him go.

While we lived in Shamokin, Daddy worked for the Russian Bible Society in Washington, DC. He went on a mission trip to Europe and Asia with two other men: Pastor Malof, who was the president of the society, and the Reverend T. Youzva. They handed out eight thousand Russian Bibles to Russian refugees. The year was 1953, during the Cold War, which made it difficult to enter and leave the Soviet Union. This was a dangerous trip for these men, since all three were from Russia. It was especially dangerous for Daddy, because although at the age of seventeen he had signed up to become a Communist, at the age of twenty-one he had fled Russia through the Underground Railroad and escaped to Canada. In Russia, when a young man reached the age of twenty-one, he was forced to enlist in the Communist Party. If they had known who Daddy was on his return trip to Russia, he would have been shot as a deserter. He would later write all about the heroic times of his escape from the Communist Party in his book called *Under the Red Star*. By the grace of God, all three men were allowed to enter Russia on this trip, and God brought them home again.

Shamokin was where I learned to ride a bike. I was five years old. There were lots of steep hills. In order to learn, I'd push my bike to the top of the hill, jump on it, and ride it down the hill. It usually worked, except one day there were deep grooves in the dirt and gravel caused by a heavy rain the previous night. When I jumped on my bike to go down the hill, my front tire got stuck in one of those deep grooves, and I rolled head over heels down the hill. Eventually I learned how to ride. However, there was one hill, covered with trees, that I was afraid to go up. The town kids said a witch lived up there in an old cabin. I did sneak up the hill once and saw the witch's cabin, but I was afraid to go any closer. It was just a small cabin, and I'm sure she was just a poor, lonely old lady.

Our next move was to Williamsport, Pennsylvania. We lived in two homes in Williamsport. The first place was a house with a finished attic. It was in this attic that Wally taught me how to whistle. I would play for hours up there with my stuffed Pop doll that Mother ordered for me from the Rice Krispies cereal box. In addition, in the backyard there was a swing set surrounded by tall cedar trees. I would swing for hours, and I always felt safe there. Right around the corner was an ice cream shop. I remember begging Mother for a nickel so I could get an ice cream cone. Times were simpler and safer back then. I've always had fond memories of that house.

Our second home in Williamsport was a vacant gymnasium attached to a church. It looked like any other gymnasium, with basketball goals on each end and with a light-colored hardwood floor. Curtains and furniture divided our rooms in this house. Mother hung white sheets around trying to make bedrooms by attaching the sheets to dresser mirrors and such. There were no permanent walls and certainly no opportunities for privacy. The gymnasium was upstairs while in the basement there was a mission for the homeless. Daddy ran the Mission Soup Kitchen, where all the homeless came. Daddy would feed them and then preach to them. He served noodles and beans, along with chicken necks and backs, all of which Mother prepared. We kids learned to find every piece of meat on those bony necks and backs. The mission board would bring us crates of clothes. We sorted through them and were happy for all the new things. From this home, I walked to school and back again. It was there that I was chased down by a boy and kissed, to which I reacted by thinking "Yuk!"

One day, Daddy brought home three baby chicks. They were so soft and fuzzy. The next morning, I woke up early just so I could hold the baby chicks. Mother and Daddy were already awake. Mother was holding her hand over her mouth in horror. "Stop," she said to me, holding out her other hand so I wouldn't come any closer. Then I saw the blood trails all over the floor. The rats had eaten the baby chicks. I knew there were rats, but I had never seen them. I certainly didn't think they would come that close to us, but they did. I was devastated.

The house I remember most was in West Stewartstown, New Hampshire. Our house was also the town library. The upstairs had a large balcony lined with books. The upstairs landing made a square around the stairs enclosed with a beautiful walnut wooden railing. Margie was in seventh heaven because she loved to read and had hundreds of books to choose from. There was a large porch on the side of the house. Mother loved the rain, as I do today, and when it rained, or even stormed, we would sit on the porch, watch the rain, and sing songs. That was when Mother taught me "Twinkle, Twinkle, Little Star." To this very day, when it rains or storms, I love to sit on the porch and sing. I taught my children the same way.

We tried to have family meals at the kitchen table when Daddy was home, but since he was a pastor and visited his congregation often, he wasn't always home. Daddy would make real German potato pancakes for breakfast. Yum! I've never had them since. There was one meal Mother made, however, that I could hardly get down, and it seemed to me that she made it all the time. It was macaroni cooked with tomatoes—no cheese! It was a fight to make me eat it every time she made it. Daddy would say, "Come here and let me see if you are full." So he would gently squeeze my head and say, "It's still soft up there, so there's still more room." With great exertion I would squint my eyes and stiffen my body as much as I could, hoping to make my head hard. Then he would say, "Now you finish your plate. There are children in Africa who are starving." I always wondered how my eating my plate full of macaroni would help them.

I was in second grade at West Stewartstown. One Halloween, our school had a contest for best costume and best disguise. Then the kids would guess who you were. Everyone was dressed up, especially Wally. He went to great lengths to cover every inch of his body so no one could guess who he was. He was dressed as a hobo, carrying a stick with a red bandana tied to the end, stuffed with clothes. I was Porky Pig. As the classes were passing one another in the hallway, I saw Wally and yelled, "Hi, Wally!" He could have killed me. Up to that time, no one could guess who he was.

New Hampshire had very cold winters. One winter, Wally and I built a snow tunnel and a snow fort. I remember it well because I froze my cheeks and they turned white as a sheet. Mother told Wally, "Go get me some snow. We're going to have to rub Josie's cheeks until the color comes back." I was sitting on the kitchen chair bawling my eyes out. Mother rubbed and rubbed my face until my cheeks felt raw. For many years after that, my cheeks would seep a clear pus every winter.

I hold many memories of West Stewartstown that mean a lot to me. In many ways, that time in my life was one of the happiest, and it was certainly important for another reason too. In that little Baptist church where Daddy preached, the Holy Spirit inspired me with His love. I was swept up in that love, almost as if for the first time, and it was in that little Baptist church that I accepted Jesus Christ as my personal Savior under Daddy's preaching.

The Houseman family: Mark, Isobel, Margaret, Josephine, Walter

Chapter 2

The Day I Got Saved

> The mercy of the Lord is from everlasting to everlasting upon them that fear him, and his righteousness unto children's children.
>
> Psalm 103:17

It was a hot June day in 1957. (This was one year before our family trip to Canada.) I was in vacation Bible school at our small Baptist church of about fifty members in West Stewartstown, New Hampshire, where my father was the pastor. I was eight years old. How I loved vacation Bible school and the smell of lacquer. The older kids got to make beautiful wooden plaques. They glued them together and painted them with shiny lacquer. I always wanted to make one of those plaques, but instead, I had to press my hand into a gooey plaster mold.

On this particular day, my father was preaching. It must have been when I reached my age of accountability, because it was the first time I really understood the gospel. (Each child's age of accountability is different.) I remember sitting in the front row, watching Daddy preach. How interesting it was. "This is really good," I remember saying to myself. I turned and looked behind me at the rest of the kids to see if they were listening, but it seemed that most of them were talking, fidgeting, or writing notes. I thought, "Why aren't they listening?"

For the first time, I realized that I was a sinner. It didn't matter that I was the preacher's daughter or that I was a good girl—I was a sinner. When the invitation was given, I went forward to be saved. A woman came and knelt with me, and I asked Jesus into my heart. I don't remember the woman's name, but I know that someday I will see her again in heaven and she will have a crown of rejoicing for leading me to the Lord. "For what is our hope, or joy, or crown of rejoicing" (1 Thessalonians 2:19). "Both he that soweth and he that reapeth may rejoice together" (John 4:36).

I was so excited; my heart felt as light as a feather. As soon as vacation Bible school was over, I ran to the house of one of my friends. For some reason she was not in Bible school that day. She lived in an apartment with lots of outside stairs, painted gray, with a front porch swing. When I got there, her mother brought us some egg salad sandwiches. I don't know what she put in those sandwiches, but they were the best-tasting egg salad sandwiches I ever had. My friend and I sat on the porch swing, and as we ate our sandwiches, I told her all about Daddy's sermon and how Jesus died on the cross for her. I told her that I had asked Jesus into my heart, and I asked, "Would you like to ask Jesus into your heart?" She said yes. We both knelt down on that porch swing, and she asked Jesus into her heart. Oh, to have childlike faith. "Suffer the little children to come unto me . . . for such is the kingdom of God" (Mark 10:14).

Prayer was always an important part of our family. I remember our family devotion time, even when I was a small child. Daddy would read the Bible, and then we would all get on our knees and pray. I remember kneeling in the living room and praying, and Mother would put her arms around me and pray with me. From when I was a small child I was taught the power of prayer. Looking back, I find great comfort in my earliest recollections of walking with Jesus. I believe the innocence of youth let me see the light more clearly than if I had lived long years without Christ in my heart. As 2 Timothy 3:15 says, "From a child thou hast known the Holy Scriptures, which are able to make thee wise unto salvation through faith which is in Christ Jesus."

Daddy was a prayer warrior. He had such a burden for souls that he would kneel at each pew and move from place to place praying for whoever might sit there on Sunday morning. He would pray that if they were not saved, they would come under conviction and the Holy Spirit would draw them unto salvation. Daddy was so full of the love of God that people said, "I see an aura about him." Daddy's godliness had a great impact on my life, and as James 5:16 tells us, "The effectual fervent prayer of a righteous man availeth much." Such was Daddy's life.

Chapter 3

Summer Of Sorrow

Precious in the sight of the Lord is the death of his saints.

Psalm 116:15

After that June of 1957 when I got saved, Daddy moved us from West Stewartstown, New Hampshire, to Berne, Indiana. The main reason was because Daddy's book, *Under the Red Star,* was being printed there by the Economy Printing Press, so Daddy felt led by the Lord to move us there. He had a dream, and in his dream he had seen a house with two peach trees in front. I remember him driving around town looking for this house he had seen in his dream. He did locate a house like the one he had seen in his dream, complete with two peach trees in front, at 418 Behring Street, Berne, Indiana, and lo and behold, it was for rent. We rented the house and moved in. I started third grade and Wally started fifth grade. Margie started eighth grade at Berne French School, which later became Berne High School.

Berne was a Swiss community with a large population of Amish. I went to school with several Amish kids. Many of the town's people had come directly over from Switzerland. It was a small, quaint community with one main street where most of the storefronts had a Swiss look about them. The store I loved the most was Berne Dime Store. It was on my way home from school, so I would always stop in and look around. The storeowners knew me by name and were friendly; they would say, "Hi Josie!" every time they saw me. My favorite place in the store was the candy shelf, and every time I had a penny or a nickel, I'd buy some candy. I was probably their best customer. There also was a grocery store, a flower shop, and two restaurants, among other stores. The First Mennonite Church was across the street from the school, and it was the largest Mennonite church in the world. Berne was a good place to live and grow up.

(Years later, however, on Palm Sunday, April 11, 1965, a tornado touched down and ripped through the main street of downtown Berne. My precious dime store was reduced to masonry rubble and piles of wood splinters the size of toothpicks. It was one of the most destructive tornados to hit the Midwest. The Berne people rebuilt the main street of downtown Berne, and this time every storefront had a Swiss look. It is more beautiful today than ever.)

Our first months living in Berne passed, and the next summer, in 1958, we took a family trip to western Canada to see Mother's relatives. Daddy had preaching engagements scheduled all the way along the route we drove. We visited Mother's aunts and uncles and stayed in their homes as we traveled from church to church. I remember one of our great-aunts, named Agnes, for whom I was given my middle name. Her fingers were all twisted with arthritis, but still she did work. Margie and I sat and watched her iron handkerchiefs and pillowcases while she told us stories about Mother when she was a child.

As I previously described, close to the end of our trip, as we were on our way to the Christian family Bible camp in the Canadian mountains near Vancouver, Daddy suffered in the July heat while driving. In addition, our car broke down. After God answered our prayers and sent what seemed to be an angel to repair our car, Daddy drove us the rest of the way to the Bible camp. But tragedy struck our family just a few days after God answered our prayers on that mountain slope. Daddy had never fully recovered from a heat stroke he had suffered earlier in California, and the extreme heat in Canada was making him sick again to the point where he could hardly stand up. Yet he never slowed down or stopped working. Four days after that terrifying experience, on Wednesday, July 30, 1958, Daddy died. His work on earth was done and the Lord called him home.

As long as I live, I shall never forget that night. We got to the camp and Daddy preached that Sunday night. It was now Wednesday and that night Daddy was going to preach at a nearby church, and as usual, all the family was supposed to go with him because we ministered in music. Daddy and Mother would sing duets, Margie would sing duets with Mother, Margie would play the accordion, and Mother would sing solos. Wally was supposed to learn the trumpet, and I was supposed to learn the violin, but we hadn't learned them enough to play in front of people yet. Daddy and Mother sang "It Is No Secret." Margie and Mother sang "Lead Me to Calvary," and Mother sang "Under His Wings." I shall never forget those beautiful songs. They shall ring in my ears forever. But for some reason, that night I got the bright idea that I wanted to be an "official camper." Where I got that idea, I'll never know. So my parents did all the necessary things and I was allowed to spend the night with the other camp girls. Then my family left for the nearby church meeting.

It turned out to be the most traumatic experience of my life. You see, as I said before, I was an "extreme" mommy's baby, and I had not been away from Mother that much except for the times we were put in different people's homes on Daddy's evangelistic trips. So, why I wanted to be a camper, I'll never know. Apparently, I thought I had grown up a little. But that night, as all the lights went out and everyone was to be quiet, I got a pain in the pit in my stomach and started to turn green. You know that terrible homesick feeling. I started crying, and I cried and cried. It wasn't long before I had everyone awake and all the camp staff trying to comfort me. The only person I wanted to see, however, was Mommy, and she wouldn't be back for hours.

Finally, a young woman of about twenty years old took me to her room and tried to console me. She gave me one of her stuffed animals to hold. It was a soft, fuzzy white cat with blue eyes. (I kept that cat until my children were born some eighteen years later.) That evening seemed like an eternity to me. Finally, Mother got back and the camp directors gladly handed me over to her. Then we all went to our cabin.

That night Daddy was extremely ill. I remember hearing him tossing and turning on his bed and moaning in our one-room cabin. Mother woke Wally up and said, "Go get help." Several men came into the room and carried Daddy out of the room on his mattress. As they were carrying him out the door, I heard one of them say, "This mattress is soaked clear through with perspiration." They put Daddy, mattress and all, in the back of an open-bed truck and took him to the hospital. Wally went with him and sat in the back of the truck. Wally says he can still remember the cold air blowing on the back of his neck. That was the last time I saw Daddy alive. In those days they did not allow children in hospitals. Daddy died in the hospital three days later from a cerebral hemorrhage, which today they call an aneurism, which is a form of stroke. "Precious in the sight of the Lord is the death of his saints" (Psalm 116:15).

The day Daddy died, we three kids were called into a small room with red brick walls and high windows. We walked in slowly. Margaret was fourteen years old, Wally was twelve, and I was nine. Mother was sitting there waiting for us with the camp director. My heart knew something terrible had happened. They told us to sit down, and then Mother said, "Daddy died." Margie started to cry immediately. I started crying because she was crying. (I don't think I understood the meaning of death yet.) Wally never cried.

Later that day, I walked to the camp restroom, which seemed to be down a lot of concrete steps. It's strange how I hadn't noticed all those steps before. Everything seemed gray and cold, and my heart was aching. There was a middle-aged woman down there, and I said to her, "My daddy just died."

She looked at me very tenderly and said, "Oh, I'm so sorry to hear that." But then she left.

I just needed someone to hold me. I don't remember anyone holding me that day. It was a very sad day, and my heart just ached with loneliness.

Walter, Josephine, Margaret, Mother and Dad. Yes, you are looking at the one's for whom you have been praying for years. All through our lives we were upheld and sustained, in much traveling, preaching, in testings and trials, all because of our faithful prayer partners. Thank God for prayer partners. Now since we became the field representatives of the **Hanbury Homes for Orphans** in Jamaica, we ever so much more depend on you, faithful co-laborers in the service of our Lord. To you who are new members to the Houseman prayer family, I would like to make known this our new step of faith. Not so long ago, I was positive I heard the Lord calling me to a different type of work. Up until August, 1957, we were nicely located as a pastor family in a lovely little church in the scenic state of New Hampshire. The Lord there spoke to me clear and plain, "Mark, move on". I said "Where to, Lord?" "Abraham went out, not knowing whither he went", was the answer. So I said, "Lord, here am I, send me." In just a few days I was over in Jamaica, B.W.I. It was here that I said to those missionaries, "Yes, I will be your field representative in the United States for the **Hanbury Homes for Orphans**". By the end of that month we moved to Berne, Indiana, into a rented home, trusting the Lord for every step we shall take. Now as your prayer object and Evangelist to many churches, I stand before you at the request of our Lord, saying to you, "Brethren, PRAY FOR US!"

As ever yours in the glorious fight for precious lost souls,

Mark Houseman

The Houseman family, 1958, the year Daddy died

Chapter 4

Life without Daddy

Thou art the helper of the fatherless.

Psalm 10:14

Mother was left alone with us three children. We traveled three days by train to bring Daddy's body to Lansing, Michigan, where his sister, Auntie Olga, lived. Daddy was to be buried there, because Mother had no money and Auntie Olga and Uncle Adolf had said that they would pay for the funeral. Olga and Adolf were the sister and brother-in-law who had helped Daddy escape Russia. They had all come to Canada together.

We entered a large room with a curtain that seemed to stretch across one entire wall, and in front of that curtain lay Daddy in a casket. It was the first time I had seen him since that dreadful night they carried him out of our cabin. Approaching the casket, Mother bent down and kissed him. All I could do was stand there and stare at him. The funeral parlor was lined with brown metal chairs, and there were people everywhere. It was a very sad day.

At the gravesite, the four of us—Mother, Margie, Wally, and I—were standing over the tombstone, which was just a small, flat granite stone. Mother looked down and there was a shiny fifty-cent piece lying on the ground. Mother picked it up and said, "This is God's way of promising He will always provide."

After the funeral, we went back to Berne and lived in the dream house Daddy had rented for us on Behring Street. We children went back to school, and since Mother was a licensed practical nurse, she got a job at the Berne Nursing Home. Life was returning to normal—somewhat.

Still, life was hard without Daddy. We had little to no money. Daddy had cancelled his whole-life insurance a few months before he died and had taken out a higher paying accident insurance, which proved to be worthless and a big mistake. But Mother did get Social Security. I walked to and from school, which was a half a mile or more from our home, in the sun, rain, and snow.

We did have our fun times. On my tenth birthday, I asked for a stuffed doggy I had seen in Berne Dime Store downtown. Mother said she couldn't afford it, which made me sad. But then on my birthday, when I opened the box, there he was: my two-toned Cocker spaniel with long, curly ears. It was a happy birthday for me.

The first Christmas without Daddy, Mother bought a silver metal Christmas tree. It had a light projector that turned, reflecting on the tree changing colors of red, blue, yellow, and green. It was so pretty. But the most beautiful Christmas tree I ever saw was at the Amstutz family's house that Christmas season. They were friends of our family and Mother was babysitting their children, and she took me along. They had an all-mauve-colored tree. I had never seen such a beautiful tree. It was flocked and had crystals everywhere, along with mauve bows and mauve lights. The lights were wrapped with glistening angel hair. It looked like a fairyland tree, and I sat and stared at it all night.

In our house at 418 Behring Street, Mother's bedroom was downstairs, while upstairs Margie and I shared one bedroom and

Wally had his own bedroom on a connecting hallway. At the top of the stairs, there was a long closet in which boxes and junk were stacked. I asked Mother, "May I straighten it up—the long closet in the hall—and use it for my dollhouse? I promise I'll keep it nice." She said that would be fine.

I spent days cleaning and rearranging that closet. When it was finished, I had my own little room where I could go to and play, read books, or just be alone. I had made a bed out of stacked boxes, which I covered with sheets and blankets. All my dolls were lined up on the bed. Other stacked boxes became my table. I covered this table with a tablecloth and put a lamp on it. I loved my little closet room. It was all my own, and I felt safe there.

I was often at home by myself while Mother was at her job. She worked the night shift from 11:00 p.m. to 7:00 a.m., but she also worked extra hours whenever permitted. Margie worked at the City Lunch Restaurant downtown, and she seemed to be gone most of the time. Wally was supposed to be watching me, but he would often leave to be with his friends. I remember calling Mother up at work and crying on the phone, begging her to come home, but of course, she couldn't, because she was the sole provider. Once I had the flu and was throwing up everywhere, and there was no one there to take care of me.

I would do anything to keep Wally home. For a while, he started making scary tapes with his tape recorder. He made Igor tapes with slamming doors, loud footsteps, and scary growls. It was my job to scream blood-curdling screams as loud as I could. Then he would call up girls he knew were home alone. He'd play the tapes on the phone, listen for their scream, and then laugh. This lasted until the police came and put a stop to his pranks.

Trying to make a more secure life for us, Mother married a man named Ellison Neuenschwander in 1961, three years after Daddy's death. I was twelve years old. We moved into my stepfather's home, a large old school house in the country, where there were no neighbors for miles. He had six children of his own, of which two still lived at home. It was a time of much adjustment; however, my brother and sister and I still went to Berne School. Unfortunately, the marriage ended in divorce six months later.

Due to the divorce and complications with Mother's health, I was sent to live in the homes of various people. The first home I was placed in was Yager Funeral Home. I had my own room with its own bath. The curtains were fancy and matched the bedspread. It was the first fancy room I had ever lived in, but that didn't matter—I felt lost and lonely and missed my family. The Yagers were kind to me; however, I became extremely quiet and withdrew into myself. I was still a mommy's baby, but instead of crying, I would just sit quietly and hold everything in. I stayed at the Yager Funeral Home for several weeks.

The next house I was placed in was Gordon Neuenschwander's home. He was the pastor of the First Mennonite Church. I stayed there for several more weeks. But I was afraid to come down and eat with them when they called me; I just stayed in my room. I know they were worried about me. I became more and more withdrawn into myself. I felt alone and afraid.

Next, I was placed in the home of Chris Muselman, the man who printed Daddy's book. I don't know who decided where I was to stay; I just went where they put me. I stayed with the Muselmans for several more weeks. They were nice, but very old, and I didn't feel comfortable with them either. I became extremely depressed and missed my family. I felt insecure and like I didn't belong anywhere.

In all three places, I walked to and from school, and when I would get to the house I would just go to my room and stay there. My distress affected my schooling too. I remember falling asleep in class once, and when they woke me up, I cried so much they sent me home. I was afraid of everyone and everything. My little secure closet room was gone, and I had no family around. I remember crying myself to sleep almost every night.

During this period when I was living in various homes, Margie moved in with her friend. Wally moved in with a friend as well. I was the only one too young to decide where I wanted to go. I know the people who took me in were simply trying to help, but to a twelve-year-old, it was devastating. I know now how foster children feel.

After a few months, Mother's health improved, and we were all brought back together as a family. It felt good to be with family again, yet emotionally I was never the same; I became very shy and quiet and felt insecure.

Chapter 5

A Friend

And thou shalt be secure, because there is hope.

Job 11:18

We could not return to Daddy's dream house, so Mother rented an upstairs apartment at 405 Water Street in Berne. It had two bedrooms. Mother, Margie, and I slept in one long bedroom, and Wally had his own. Mother continued working at Berne Nursing Home, and we enjoyed the apartment. Margie still worked at the restaurant downtown, and she finished her senior year at Berne High School. Wally went to school and did farm work in the summer. Our home now was only one block from school, so it was easy for me to walk to and from school. I was thirteen years old, Wally was sixteen, and Margie was eighteen. She planned to go on in the fall to Ball State Teachers College, which later became Ball State University.

Growing up without Daddy and the experience of living in different people's homes caused me to become insecure. I was a Christian and tried to trust in the Lord, but I was not dedicated to living a godly Christian life. Yes, I attended church; I was active in the Youth for Christ Club at school; and I didn't run around with wild kids. Deep down in my heart, however, I knew I was not what God wanted me to be. But God, in His marvelous wisdom, gave me a Christian friend, Linda Zuercher.

Linda and I became closer than sisters. We were both fourteen years old and in the ninth grade, and it wasn't long before we became bosom buddies. God used Linda to help me through my feelings of awkwardness and insecurity. She accepted me as I was. I could be myself around her and not be afraid of being criticized or made fun of. I could confide in her, knowing she would not betray my trust. We were true kindred spirits. We had such good times with each other. We laughed together, cried together, and shared our secrets and innermost thoughts and fears. God knew I needed her, and her mother, Lucille, said Linda needed me.

Linda felt like everything she loved was taken away from her, or died—mainly her pets. Like me, she felt lonely and insecure, though I don't think she was as insecure as I was. Linda was more hyperactive than I was, and because I was quiet, her mother said I calmed her down. Lucille said Linda and I complemented each other. Linda and I were more like sisters than friends. Our relationship was rare and special—a gift given by God, who knew we both needed each other.

We did crazy little things like walking down the railroad track with our arms around each other, marching stiff legged and harmonizing as we sang:

> We ain't got a barrel of money.
> Maybe we're ragged and funny,
> But we'll travel along,
> Singing our song,
> Side by side.

One time we buried a secret walnut under the cottonwood tree in her backyard. In the hollowed-out walnut, we put a lucky penny and a note with the names of the boys we liked. Then we vowed to dig it up "exactly" one year later. I remember how excited I felt when we dug it up. We had both forgotten what we wrote. After opening the walnut and reading the note we'd written, we looked at each other and said, "Yuk! How could we have liked those creeps?"

Linda and I wore clothes alike, combed our hair alike, and were hardly ever seen apart. The kids at school called us the Bobbsey Twins. On the days Linda was sick, I didn't want go to school and felt sad and lonely. We bought identical real gold cross necklaces and gave them to each other, and we vowed to keep them forever. Fifty years later, we each still have them; every time I look at mine, it reminds me of Linda.

As girls, we both showed a curious and adventurous spirit. One day we rode our bikes to an abandoned barn. We got off our bikes and walked through the tall grass that hadn't been mowed for a long time, making sure we didn't run into any black widow spiders. We went into the barn and walked around. It was old and decayed. While we were on the ground floor, the wooden boards gave way and I fell through. I grabbed hold of some old boards and was hanging by my arm, screaming. Linda ran down to the lower level, which was full of water, concrete blocks, and old lumber. She grabbed my legs and pushed me up by my feet until I could get out of the hole in the floor. We could have really been hurt that day, but I guess our guardian angels were working overtime to protect us.

When Linda was at my house, her mother would come pick her up. When I was at Linda's house, her mother would take me home. At my house, which was the upstairs apartment, we would wait for her mother on the inside staircase. Sometimes, if it was snowing, we'd go out in the yard and make snow angels or pretend to be trees. Every time a car would pass we would stiffen and stop moving, with our arms out and our head cocked, looking frozen. I'm sure we were a funny sight.

When I was at her house, we would sit in front of a large bush they had in their front yard and wait for her mother to get the car out of the garage and come around and pick me up and take me home. Sometimes we would go out to the bush and just sit there for hours and share our innermost thoughts and dreams. I wrote a poem about the stairs (which we can't find) and Linda wrote a poem about the bush. Here is Linda's poem that she wrote in 1963:

The Bush

This bush has a nice story to tell,
Of two friends that learned to love each other well.
When they were kids they would sit by this bush together,
And made a wish to be friends FOREVER.
They would laugh and talk together,
And dream of things that couldn't come true, ever.
When the sun would set and the stars appeared in the sky
The two very close friends would have to say good-bye.
But these friends knew their fun wouldn't always last forever.
They were sad because they were a part of one another.
They dreaded the day they would have to leave.
But they would always remember the fun they had by the bush
And the wonderful memories they had received.
The years flew by just too fast
And those togetherness days were gone at last.
And when they would gaze at the sunset,
It would bring them back to the past,
And how their life was going by so fast.

Yes! Those two were the closest of friends.
Their true love for each other will never end.
They had something more precious than money could ever be.
You see, I ought to know, one of those friends was me.

I thank God for giving me such a friend. Linda was a true gift from God. We had—and still do have—a true friendship that few ever find in a lifetime.

In the year 1964, at the age of fifteen, I had to have oral surgery on my mouth. My two eyeteeth had never come in, and I still had my baby teeth. X-rays revealed that they were still in the roof of my mouth, but they were lying on their side and abscessed. Mother took me to a specialist, and surgery was scheduled at Lutheran Hospital in Fort Wayne.

In my room at the hospital, there was another girl, about my age. She was going to have oral surgery also. The night before our surgery, we were supposed to stay in our room, but the girl said she wanted to go for a walk down the hall. Mother was with me at the hospital, and she said I could go. But instead of just walking down the hall, the girl ended up going far away from our room, looking for cute orderlies. I was lost and just followed her.

As we passed a particular hospital room, a man called us into his room. He too was a patient. He was in his pajamas. He said, "What are you girls doing?"

"We're looking for orderlies," we said.

Then he asked us, "How old are you?" We told him we were 19.

He asked us to sign his personal guest book, which we did, and beside our names he put a question mark and wrote, "They say they are 19?"

While we were running around the hospital looking for orderlies, the nurses were running around looking for us to give us our sleeping pill. They finally found us and made us lie down and go to sleep.

My surgery took four hours, and there were some complications. When they brought me back to my room, Mother was still there. She stayed all night with me, sleeping in a chair. I had lost a lot of blood, which had gone down into my stomach. Thank God that Mother was there, because in the middle of the night I threw up a full pail of blood and fainted. I was too weak to call the nurse or even push the button for help. Mother said that I would have fallen out of bed on my head if she had not been there. In my operation they had cut the roof of my mouth along the entire line of my teeth, from front to back. Then they peeled my roof clear back. I was so abscessed that they had to drain it first. I had fifteen stitches.

After two days in the hospital, Mother brought me home. I could eat only three-minute soft-boiled eggs—no sucking or chewing, which made it very difficult. I kept my mouth shut, because if I opened it even a little, the dried blood smelled so bad that it nearly knocked everyone out.

Mother put me in the bathtub and helped me bathe. When I stood up, everything went to black and white fuzz like a TV on the blink, and I fainted. Thank God, Mother was there for me.

Later, sitting alone on my bed, looking out the tall, thin window beside me, I read my Bible. I came to Psalm 19:14, which says, "Let the words of my mouth and the meditation of my heart be acceptable in thy sight, O Lord, my strength and my redeemer." It seemed so appropriate, because I could not speak or even open my mouth. All I could do was pray and meditate on God's Word. I wanted my mouth to be clean and my heart to be pure before God. I believe that throughout my childhood there were times when God gave me a glimpse of Himself. I can look back on those times as periods of spiritual growth. This was one of those times. I remember feeling a warmth and peace in my heart and security in Christ. That night I memorized Psalm 19:14 and it became my life's verse from then on.

I truly felt close to Jesus when I was first saved as a child under my father's ministry, but the intervening years of tragedy, hardship, loneliness, and sadness caused me to inch away from my initial true love for Christ. My sincere heart's desire was to have a close, intimate relationship with God. However, even through all this, I didn't become serious about living for God and having a daily devotional prayer life.

Linda, 1967

Josie, 1967

The bush

Chapter 6
Life-Changing Decisions

Show me thy ways, O Lord; teach me thy paths.

Psalm 25:4

My time with Linda almost came to an abrupt end in 1964, making that year memorable on many levels. By that time, we had lived in the upstairs apartment on Water Street for three years. I had just finished my sophomore year at Berne High School. Margie was a sophomore at Ball State University and was preparing to be married to Ed Bunsold from Winchester, Indiana. The year before, Walter had married Sandy, and they had lived with us in the apartment for a year. At the time that Walter finished his senior year and graduated in 1964, they were about to have their first baby. So Mother bought them a trailer in Geneva, Indiana, in which they lived.

I don't know why, but it was at this time that Mother accepted a job in Fort Wayne, Indiana, as a live-in maid and nanny for the household of Earl Wells, the manager of the zoo at Franke Park. She was going to let go of the upstairs apartment and move to Fort Wayne. But that left me in a crisis. I was still 15 at the time, not old enough to live by myself yet, and I didn't want to be uprooted again and leave all my friends, especially Linda. Besides, my mother wouldn't be moving us into our own home; we would just be staying in a room at Earl Wells' house. I would have to change schools, from a small-town school to a large-city school. It would mean starting all over again. I told Mother that I didn't want to go. I didn't know what to do. I was at a loss. But looking back, I can see God's hand at work in my life.

Mother accepted the position and moved to Fort Wayne. I told her I didn't want to go to Fort Wayne. Because she had just bought Walter and Sandy a new trailer, Mother decided to move me in with them in nearby Geneva, so I could continue attending Berne High School. Sandy had just had the baby, so I was to help with the baby and be a built-in babysitter. Things went okay for the first few months. But it is never good to put another person in with a newly married couple.

One day Sandy and I had an argument, and I ran out the door and hid behind the wheel of the trailer. Sandy yelled, "Josephine, get back in this house!" I wasn't about to go back in that house. I waited until she had gone inside and shut the door. Then I started walking downtown to the Geneva grocery store, where I knew there was a phone.

It was winter and it had just begun to snow. I had no coat, and it was a mile or more to the grocery store. By the time I got there, I was frozen. I called Linda and asked her if her mother could come pick me up. They arrived about forty-five minutes later and took me to their home. I remember sitting on the edge of the bed in the study, crying, not knowing what to do. Linda said, "Oh Mother, can she live with us?"

Lucille looked at me with compassion in her eyes and said, "Yes, she can live with us." Lucille later said that at that moment the Lord had laid a burden on her heart for me.

This was a big sacrifice for them, because the Zuerchers had five children of their own: Margaret, who was married and out of the house; Paul, who was a senior in high school; Linda, who was my age; Elaine, who was about twelve years old; and Leon, who was five years old. It was the Lord who opened this door for me, because at that time in my life I really needed spiritual guidance and discipline. He knows our needs before we ask.

So Walter and Lucille Zuercher took me into their home. If it hadn't been for them heeding the prompting of the Holy Spirit and accepting the responsibility of taking a teenage girl into their home, I don't know where I would be today. While living there I was able to observe Lucille, who was an obedient and submissive wife to her husband. I'm not saying that Mother wasn't submissive to Daddy, for she was, but it was now going on six years—from the age of nine through fifteen—that I had missed out on Daddy's godly influence in the home. After all the turmoil and hardships I had endured so far, I needed stability and guidance in my life.

Lucille was one of the godliest women I have known. I observed her daily giving loving devotion to her husband and children. In addition, she was always helping others in any way she could. I heard her say "Thank you Jesus" for everything, even a parking place. Her loving ways put a longing in my heart to be like her. I so wanted to have a gentle spirit and be soft spoken like she was. God used Lucille to put a desire in my heart to be godly like her. She was definitely a Proverbs 31 woman. "Who can find a virtuous woman? For her price is far above rubies. Her children shall rise up and call her blessed" (Proverbs 31:1).

I stayed in the Zuerchers' home for two and a half years, including my junior and senior years in high school. Unknown to me, God was using them to direct and engineer my paths. "Trust in the Lord with all thine heart and lean not unto thine own understanding. In all thy ways acknowledge him, and he shall direct thy paths" (Proverbs 3:4-5).

It was nice living at the Zuerchers' home, because Linda was there. They started us off in the same room, but that didn't work because Linda and I talked and giggled all night and neither we nor they got any sleep, so they separated us. I stayed in Elaine's room and Linda moved into the study.

Linda's mother always drove her to school, so that meant no more walking for me. It seemed like it was always a rush to get to the car in time to leave for school. If we didn't have time for breakfast, Linda would grab a piece of bread—no butter, just bread—and eat it on the way to school. I learned that bread tasted pretty good. We took all our classes together and always sat next to each other in class. When we were walking down the hall, the kids knew that if they saw one, the other couldn't be far behind. Both Linda and I loved to draw. So we became the official poster makers for all the school events.

Living at Linda's house was like being at a slumber party every night. We were still our silly selves. We studied together, played records together, and stood in front of the mirror and put on makeup together. We were inseparable. Once we both had our hair done at the beauty parlor for our school pictures to be taken the next day. We didn't want our hairdos to be crushed, so we sat up all night watching scary movies.

Hardly ever did Linda and I fight. I only remember one time, and it was over a boy, of course. It was Saturday, which was dishwashing day. Sometime after our fight, Lucille called me to dry the dishes. I came and dried for my length of time. Then Lucille told me to go get Linda for her turn. I said, "That's okay; I'll take her turn too." Lucille stopped and looked at me and said, "Blessed are the peacemakers." I shall never forget that. It really spoke volumes to my soul. When the dishes were done, I went back to my room, and there on my bed was a note, which said, "I'm sorry. Love, Linda." That's the type of friendship we had.

The Lord placed Linda and Lucille in my life at the time He knew I needed friendship, understanding, acceptance, and love.

Walter and Lucille Zuercher

Chapter 7

Worldly Influences

Beware lest any man spoil you through philosophy and vain deceit, after the tradition of men, and after the rudiments of the world, and not after Christ.

Colossians 2:8

The years with Linda were very important to me. I felt safe in her home, and I felt a growing companionship with Jesus. Yet the travails in my life did continue. Linda's family went on vacation every summer, and I wasn't invited to accompany them, which meant having to go live with my mother in Fort Wayne, where she was the live-in housekeeper for Earl Wells and his children. So I was uprooted again. Earl Wells was divorced and had the care of the children, which included a three-year-old boy named Bradley and two teenagers. Mother had a small bedroom to call her own. She and I had to sleep in the same bed, because that's all there was. We shared the bathroom with the family of four, which made it difficult. I never felt at home there. Mother was chief cook and bottle washer. The kids never cleaned up after themselves; they left it for Mother to clean up.

I was sixteen by this time, so I had to find a job. My first job was selling magazines door to door. Mother had a car, so I drove her car to work. The magazine company would drop me off at a residential area, saying that they would be back in two hours to pick me up and take me to another area. Order sheets were all I carried. I was totally alone and on my own. I had a lot of doors slammed in my face, and wow, what a feeling of rejection. They didn't have bottled water or cell phones back then, and there were times I got so tired and thirsty I thought I was going to faint.

Believe me: my guardian angel had to be working overtime again. At one house a cute young guy came to the door. He invited me in for a bottle of soda pop. He seemed nice enough, and a bottle of pop sounded good, so I went in. The house, in a rich neighborhood, was big and beautiful. He said he wanted to show me around, so I followed him from room to room as he showed me all his collections of things.

Then he went upstairs. I was so innocent and naïve that I followed him. He went into his bedroom, sat on the bed, and said, "Sit down, you must be tired." I just stood there staring at him and starting to feel scared. Suddenly the front door opened downstairs and a voice said, "We're home."

"Thank God," I thought. I quickly left. God protected me that day. I had been totally unaware of the grave danger I was in.

I figured out that I wasn't good at selling magazines. I didn't even sell one. I told the magazine people what had happened, so the next day they sent me out with a young man who was also in their employment. After walking from house to house, we decided to rest a bit in a nearby park. As we sat there, he saw a Huddle House restaurant in the distance. He said, "Hey, let's go get something to drink." I remember we had to cross a field and a creek to get there, but we finally made it. We were hot and sweaty.

We sat at the counter. He was more outspoken then I was, and he asked if there were any job openings available. They said they needed a busboy and a waitress. We filled out the applications right then and were hired on the spot. He became the busboy and I became a waitress. The next day we both quit the magazine job.

I knew nothing of waitress work, but I soon learned. And I also learned that you had to watch your back or some guy would pat you on the bottom. The Huddle House seemed to be the "wild spot" of Fort Wayne, because it stayed open twenty-four hours. Sometimes I had to work the night shift, and oh boy, nights were a whole different world.

I stayed away from any form of wildness as much as I could, but Mother didn't have a home church and Earl Wells and his family didn't go to church. This caused me to have sort of a relapse in my closeness to God. I had previously drawn closer to God through my fellowship with Linda and her mother, but living in Fort Wayne inched me away again. In the first week in which I had moved in at Earl Wells's house, I had told Mother that I was going to use that summer to read through the entire Bible. That didn't happen, because I became spiritually weakened by worldly influences. I wasn't rooted and grounded in God's Word yet. I loved Mother and was happy to be with her, but I was glad when school resumed in the fall and I could return to the Zuercher home, where there was some sort of discipline and there were rules.

Linda and I attended the First Mennonite Church, where all in her family were members. We became involved in Sunday school. We also sang in the Messiah concert under Dr. Freeman Burkhalter. That in itself was an amazing experience. I felt at home with the Zuercher family. Yet there was always an emptiness as I longed for my family. I knew I didn't truly belong. I remember once I was so depressed that I sat on my bed and bawled. Lucille came in and held me and said, "I know this is hard for you, but someday you will have your own home and your own family." That seemed like a dream, far away. If it hadn't been for Lucille's motherly love, I don't think I would have made it through that difficult time. She was truly a gift sent by God to give me stability and direction in my life. I thank God for her, and I love her for it.

During my senior year in high school, the Zuerchers sent Linda and me to Washington, DC, for a Youth for Christ rally with Bill Bright. During the rally, God got ahold of my heart, and I surrendered my life to His service. It was an evening service in a large arena with all the lights dimmed. You could see only the stage in front, where Bill Bright and the song leaders were. I sat at the far back. At the end of the service, they asked anyone to stand up who was really sincere about surrendering their life to God's service. I stood up immediately, not looking around. That night there was a real change in my life.

I started having regular daily devotional times and started praying more about daily concerns. Even Linda said she could see a big change in me. Had it not been for God's intervention that allowed me to live in the Zuerchers' home at this time in my life, I would have missed out on God's dealing with my heart and drawing me closer to Him to fulfill His purposes in my life.

My senior year went by quickly, and soon it was time to graduate from high school with the class of 1967. I was seventeen years old. My high school was called Berne High School until my senior year, when it was consolidated with Geneva High School, our arch enemy and rival in all sport events. The new school name became South Adams High School. It was our class who got to choose the new school colors and mascot. Berne High School's colors were blue and white, and the mascot was a bear—the Berne Bears. Our class chose yellow and white as the new school colors and Starfires as the mascot. I didn't vote for either one. I wanted red and white Tigers, but yellow and white Starfires won the vote. We were the first class to graduate from South Adams High School.

However, after graduation I was uprooted again and had to return to Fort Wayne and work once again at the Huddle House restaurant. Only this time, I became deathly sick with bronchitis.

Here is what led to the bronchitis: Just before summer started, Linda and I had gone to a church camp. She and I took a boat out on the lake and we both fell asleep. When we woke up, we were badly sunburned and very hungry. When we got back to shore, we found we had missed supper. Being so hungry, we sneaked into the kitchen to see if there was any food left. It had all been put away, so we went into the walk-in freezer and foraged for whatever we could find. Because I was so hot and sweaty, the cold temperature of the freezer made me sick with bronchitis.

The Huddle House had to let me go because I was coughing so much. I spent most of that summer in bed being nursed by Mother. Looking back, perhaps God allowed me to become sick with bronchitis in order to protect me from worldly influences.

Plans were made, and I was accepted at Ball State University for the upcoming year.

Chapter 8

College Days

*In all thy ways acknowledge him
and he shall direct thy paths.*

Proverbs 3:6

I started classes at Ball State University in the fall of 1967, pursuing a major in elementary education. Even the way I settled on my choice of major was a miracle. During orientation, all the students were to meet with their counselor. There were four lines and hundreds of kids. I got in a line and stood there for hours. When it was finally my turn, it just so happened that the counselor I got knew Margie, my sister. Earlier that year, I had chosen social work as my major. When my counselor, whom I hadn't previously known, heard what my major was, he said, "You don't want to be a social worker. You want to be a teacher like your sister." I took his advice, and he changed all my classes to an elementary education major. That was a miracle. If it had been any other counselor, they would not have cared what major I had and would have just enrolled me in the classes. There were four lines of students, and God directed me to this counselor. God intervened that day and directed my paths.

Linda was accepted at Bob Jones University in South Carolina. So I was going to lose my best friend and would have to start all over again. The night before school began, I stayed with Margie and Ed, who had been married for a year by then. They took me out to dinner and to a movie. They came with me to my dormitory, LaFollette, which was a brand new dorm that year. They stayed a while and helped me get settled in. The only problem was that the dorm hadn't officially opened yet. I had been given permission to move in early because Margie and Ed both had to be at work the next day. So they took me a day early. All the rest of the kids wouldn't arrive until the next day. I was alone that night in the dormitory with all those empty rooms. It was scary and lonely. I cried myself to sleep.

As the school year proceeded, weekends and holidays came; when I wanted to take a break from the campus, I had no place to go except Margie and Ed's. Mother had left her position in Fort Wayne and had moved to Muncie, where she took another position as a live-in nanny, but there was no place for me there. After the experience of living with Walter and Sandy, I decided it would be best if I stayed at school through the weekends. But I did spend special holidays with Margie and Ed, which was always fun.

My roommate was named Sue. She and I became friends, but we never became close. I had a few dates during the school year, but nothing ever came of them. Close to the end of that year, in the last week of May 1968, I received an invitation to go on a blind date. It would also be a double date with Barb and her boyfriend, Steve. Barb was a girl who lived in the room next to mine. She said that Steve's car had broken down and that he had asked one of his friends to bring him up to see her at the university. Steve's friend had said he would, but only if they set him up with a blind date. She asked me, "Will you be his blind date?"

I never had a blind date before, so I was a little reserved, but I said, "Okay, as long as you promise me that he is cute."

Answered Prayer

The night of the blind date, Barb and I were looking out the dorm window to see if we could see them. They parked right below our window, and we watched them walk into the building. The one with the car was tall, with dark hair. We met at the front desk and he said, "Hi, my name is Marvin Blocher."

He had black hair and bright blue eyes with long black eyelashes. I thought to myself, "Wow, he is cute!" It was love at first sight. On our first date, which was a double date, we went to the Hullabaloo and then to a drive-in movie.

First was the dancing at the Hullabaloo. I really had never danced before. When I went to the junior and senior prom, Berne High School didn't have dancing, so I didn't know how to dance. Marvin, however, was a good dancer and did all kinds of special moves. But because the form of dancing back then was "The Twist," I simply watched Barb and caught on pretty quick.

After the movie we all went to Ball State University to see the "Benny." The Benny is an angel statue in the middle of the campus. I told Marvin, "Legend has it that anyone who kisses behind the Benny gets married." I told him that Ed gave Margie her diamond in front of the Benny. Marvin took me behind the Benny and kissed me. I felt swept off my feet. It was late when the boys got us back to the dorm, and the dorm doors were locked because we had missed curfew. So we had to go to the dean's office and get permission to be allowed in.

Marvin asked me if he could see me again. Then he said, "Next time, I'll come in my old beat-up truck." I said that would be okay. That made all the difference in the world to him, because there were a lot of girls who wanted to date him because of his souped-up car. He had a 1967 red GTO Sprint with a four on the floor. But I didn't care what he drove. I wasn't used to fancy things anyway, and an old beat-up truck would be fine with me.

"Beneficence" statue on the Ball State campus. THE STAR PRESS FILE PHOTO

Benny

Our blind date was just before school ended. I had to be out of the dorm by the end of that week. Walter and Sandy weren't together anymore, so Mother had rented him a small apartment over a garage on Tenth Street in Anderson. I moved in with him. I had lived there less than a week when Walter joined the Marines.

The Vietnam War was in full swing at this time. Walter's marriage to Sandy had failed, ending in divorce. He was twenty-one years old at this point, and he too had endured a hard life since Daddy died. He always had been somewhat of a rebel. He wrote his autobiography many years later, called *Born to Be a Rebel*. When he enlisted in the Marines, I was sad to see him go, only because I was alone again. He was shipped to Vietnam. When he returned home two years later, he seemed to be okay and not too messed up like a lot of the men that came home from Vietnam. Soon after he came back, he moved to California and married Rhonda; they had two children.

Later that week, Barb came over to my apartment above the garage and said Marvin wanted to see me again. She asked, "Would you like to go on another double date with Steve and me?" I said that would be great. Then Barb also told me, "He might ask you to come home with him for the weekend to meet his parents." Marvin lived in North Manchester, which was a two-hour drive one way. Well, I was alone anyway, and a weekend trip sounded good to me, so I packed a suitcase and hid it under my bed just in case he did ask.

When they all got there, Marvin said, "Would you be interested in coming home with me for the weekend to meet my parents and you could stay with them?"

I quickly ran to the bed, pulled out my suitcase, and said, "I'm ready!"

Marvin just stared at me in shock. He said, "Is there anybody we need to ask?"

I said, "No." Then I added, "Well, I guess I could let my mother know." At that time she was a live-in worker at a boys' reformatory in Anderson. We drove out there, and I introduced her to Marvin. I told her that I was going home with him for the weekend to North Manchester and that I would be staying with his parents. She said okay.

Later that night, I met Marvin's parents. It was agreed I would be staying with them, while Marvin would return to the house he owned downtown. As Marvin and I were walking back to his car for him to leave, I said, "I've seen your father before, in those pajamas."

Marvin said, "Sure!" But in the back of his mind he was thinking, "Oh, boy, I've got a nut case." At that time I couldn't remember where I had seen his father, but I knew I had seen him. Marvin and I got married several months after this occurrence. Two years after we were married, his dad found the guest book I had signed in Lutheran Hospital, with the words and question mark beside my signature, reading, "They say they are 19?" I was fifteen at that time, but I was truly nineteen when I later met him with Marvin. I met the father of the man I was to marry four years before I met the man. God truly works in mysterious ways. Yet, for a child of God, nothing is happenstance. God is engineering our circumstances and directing our paths.

Chapter 9
A New Beginning

Be ye not unequally yoked together with unbelievers . . .

2 Corinthians 6:14

North Manchester was a farming community, and Marvin's parents, Jonas and Alpha Blocher, owned a forty-acre farm and milked forty-five head of dairy cattle. They also raised chickens. I ended up staying with them for the summer. Marvin had an older brother named Marion, an older sister named Mary Elizabeth, and a younger sister named Marlene. The Blochers were well known in North Manchester, because Samuel Blocher, Marvin's grandfather, had previously owned most of the west side of the town. Marvin's uncles and cousins were large farmers in the community. There were many uncles and cousins around.

Indeed, it seemed there were Blochers everywhere. This was something I was not used to, but I really liked the idea of a large extended family. Everybody was related to everybody, and they were all happy to meet me.

Most of the Blochers were German Baptist; however, Marvin's parents left the church when he was small, so they were no longer of the German Baptist faith. They were still accepted by the

German Baptist people, however, because they were considered family.

It just so happened that in that year the German Baptist annual meeting was being held in North Manchester. German Baptists came from all across the United States and Canada to the meeting. It lasted for two weeks. The men would come in, take down all the fences of the hosting farmer, and put up large tents in order to accommodate the annual meetings and meals for five thousand or more people. The meals always consisted of beef and noodles, mashed potatoes, homemade bread, and homemade apple butter. They housed the people by putting up bunk beds in all the barns, chicken houses, and outbuildings. When the annual meeting was over, the men replaced all the fences, planted all the crops, and painted all the buildings.

When my mother found out that I was staying in North Manchester, she also moved there and became a full-time live-in maid at the downtown hotel. I felt sorry for her because it seemed that since Daddy died she had never had a home of her own. Daddy's death affected us all. But not long after Mother moved to North Manchester she met Lawrence Conley. They were married, and a few years later they moved to California, close to Walter and Rhonda.

While dating during my teenage years, I had never paid that much attention to make sure that I only dated Christian boys. Yet I would always witness to them and take them to church. After dating Marvin for a while, I knew he wasn't saved. But I just overlooked it. While I had been living in the dorm at Ball State, I became a member of Grace Baptist Church in Anderson, pastored by Don Camp. I asked Marvin to go to church with me in Anderson and meet my pastor.

On July 14, 1968, Marvin and I visited Grace Baptist Church. It was a Sunday morning, and Pastor Camp preached a salvation message. During the invitation, he asked everyone to bow their heads and close their eyes. While my eyes were still closed, I heard a rustling noise beside me. I opened my eyes, and there was Marvin walking down the aisle to be saved. What a surprise, and what a blessing. He was baptized that same evening. The next Sunday we went back and he joined the church. Two weeks later Marvin asked me to marry him. I said yes.

Even as my father's body lay in the grave, my father's prayers were being answered. One of his constant prayers had been that his children would marry Christian mates. My husband-to-be was saved two months before we were married.

I was well aware that Marvin and I had not known each other for very long (we became engaged about two months after we met), but I needed a home and someone to love me and take care of me. So when Marvin said he wanted to marry me, I latched on to him and stuck like glue. We were both nineteen years old. Plans were made, and we set the date for September 22, 1968, at Grace Baptist Church to be married by Pastor Don Camp. Marvin's mother made my wedding dress and all the bridesmaids' dresses. My mother hired the caterers and did all the necessary plans.

The day came for me to walk down the aisle and to be given away by Walter Zuercher. All of us ladies—Mother, Marvin's mother, Lucille, my bridesmaids, Margie, and Barb, and my maid of honor, Linda—were in the nursery getting dressed and doing last-minute things. I went into the bathroom, shut the door, and just bawled. I looked straight into the mirror and said, "You've done it now, Josephine. You don't even know this man." I wanted to back out, but when I thought of all the planning and all the people, including all of Marvin's German Baptist relatives who had come down from Goshen, Indiana, I knew I had to go through with it. Once I saw Marvin standing at the altar, smiling at me while I walked down the aisle, all my fears vanished.

It rained all that day. During the wedding ceremony, at the moment when the pastor finished saying "If there be any reason this couple should not be joined together in holy matrimony, let him speak now or forever hold his peace," a lightning bolt struck and the lights flickered.

I thought, "Oh boy, I hope that's a good sign."

Marvin owned his own home in downtown North Manchester at 402 South Half Street, so we were going to live there. That night, after the wedding, we went to our home and we were "belled." Some of Marvin's family came over, tapped on the windows, and scared us. Then they came into the house and made us open up all our presents, because we hadn't opened them at the church. When they finally left around 2:00 a.m., I went and turned down the bed. They had filled it with pine cones, pine needles, corn, rocks, and dirt. So I had to change the sheets. It was not fun. At least they didn't take us out in the back of a pickup truck and drive us around till morning, which is what they sometimes do. Belling still is a German Baptist custom.

We did not have a honeymoon, because we couldn't afford it. I had transferred from Ball State University to Manchester College. Therefore, on the day after our wedding, a Monday, I started Manchester College and Marvin returned to work. He was a tool and die operator at the Grip-Co factory in South Whitley. We were both exhausted because of being belled.

Our first year of marriage was tough financially, but Marvin worked three jobs to put me through college. His first job was at Grip-Co factory, where he was a tool and die operator and was in line for the foremanship. That was his main job. His second job was at Peabody Seating Company, where he welded school desks and chairs and became head line-lead man. He had worked for Peabody Seating Company for several years before and was such a good welder that they sent him to Detroit and Pontiac, Michigan to repair the school desks and chairs that had been destroyed during the riots of 1966. His third job was working three nights a week on the midnight shift catching chickens for Strauss Feeding Company. I remember him coming home at three in the morning from catching chickens and having to get up at 6:00 a.m. to go back to work at Grip-Co. He'd wake up and say, "What day is it? What time is it? What job do I go to next?" Marvin was a hard worker and did whatever was necessary to bring in the income.

September 22, 1968

Chapter 10

Our First Year

And they shall be one flesh.

Genesis 2:24

Our first year of marriage was a learning experience for both of us. Since I had never really had a stable home since Daddy died, I had never learned to cook. The only thing I knew how to cook was goulash. Most of the time, I had just opened a can of tuna fish. Well, now I had a hungry man to feed. Immediately, I set to the job of rearranging the home and furniture, which was my specialty. Lucille was right; it was a wonderful feeling to have my own home.

Marvin didn't have many kitchen things, so we purchased dishes and silverware, pots and pans, and whatever we needed to set up house and didn't get as a wedding gift. We settled on plastic dishes and plastic cups, which I didn't like, but because of cost, that was all we could afford.

As I was arranging my kitchen, I ended up with a handful of paper sacks. All my cabinets were full, and I had no place to put them. I held the sacks in my arms and turned around in a circle, looking for the perfect place. You see, I was (and still am) a perfectionist. Everything has to have a place, and everything has to be in its place. I was saying to myself, "Where would be a good place to put these sacks?" Then I saw a bottom drawer in the stove. "Perfect," I said. So I stuffed all the paper sacks in the bottom of the stove. I didn't know how to cook, and I certainly had never cooked on a gas stove before.

Later, the first time I lit the oven, the entire stove caught on fire. I started screaming. Marvin ran in, grabbed the fire extinguisher, and put the fire out. He said, "What happened?" I told him about the sacks. He couldn't believe I would put paper sacks in the bottom of a gas stove.

Another time when I was going to make dinner, Marvin said, "Just make something simple, like egg sandwiches." To me, egg sandwiches were not simple, but I wanted to please my husband. So I boiled the eggs, waited for them to cool, mixed them with mayonnaise and relish, and spread it on bread. This whole time Marvin was thinking, "What is taking so long?" But he didn't want to upset his new wife, so he didn't say anything. After about forty-five minutes, I brought out the egg salad sandwiches. He looked at them and said, "I just meant fried eggs with mayonnaise on bread." I had never heard of fried egg sandwiches, but I soon learned.

A little while later, I wanted to make a pumpkin pie. I bought the piecrust and a can of pumpkin filling. I had never made any pie before, let alone pumpkin pie, so I just opened the can and dumped the pumpkin mix into the crust. After I baked it for four hours, it still wasn't done. When Marvin came home, I brought out a pie with a charcoal crust and an uncooked pumpkin center. He just looked at it in amazement.

On another occasion, I wanted to cook one of his favorite recipes, so I got his mother's recipe for meatloaf he said he liked. I followed the recipe to the letter, except when it came to how much salt to put in—I mistook her "t." for a "c." I put in two cups of

Answered Prayer

salt. When Marvin got home, he said, "Yum, that looks good." I waited with anticipation for his first bite. He took one bite. His eyes got big, his face turned green, and he spit out the meatloaf.

I ran to the bedroom and threw myself on the bed, bawling. I said, "I try so hard, and everything I do turns out awful."

Marvin sat on the bed and held me. He said, "Don't cry, Honey. From now on, whatever you fix I'll eat."

By the end of that year, he was in the hospital with an inflamed stomach. The doctor's prescription was, "Buy your wife a cookbook." I've learned to cook some, but if it doesn't come in a box or a can, I don't fix it.

Soon after we were married, I wanted some type of pet. Marvin got me a black and white cat that I named Angie. The only problem was she was pregnant. Soon after we got her, she had kittens in our closet. Talk about a mess! It wasn't long before I had six baby kittens climbing my curtains and tearing up my couch with their claws. We gave the kittens and Angie away.

Then Marvin brought home a cat he found roaming around the Grip-Co factory where he worked. It was a gray tiger-striped cat. I named him Pharaoh, because he reminded me of the cats you see in pictures on Egyptian walls. Actually, he was more like a lynx than a cat. He had pointed ears with black hairs at the top that came up into a peak, and he had a bobbed tail. He would roam around the house at night with eerie growls that sounded like a bobcat. I was scared to death of him. I was afraid he'd kill us in our sleep.

Late one night, around 2:00 a.m., Pharaoh was crouched down in the window, clawing the wooden sill and growling over and over again with a blood-curdling cry. I thought he had turned rabid. We called the police. They came and shot him with a dart gun. After they shot him, he jumped straight at them. I've never seen two policemen move so fast. Finally, the dart took effect and the police took him away. I never wanted another cat after that.

Our house was old and had a lot of critters. Because Marvin worked nights, I was alone at night. One night, several mice were running around the house, and they became so brave that they would run out right in front of me. When Marvin came home, he found me asleep in the bed with the broom in my hand. When he touched me to wake me up, I swung the broom at him, thinking he was a mouse.

The house also had bats. Once, we were watching TV with some friends when we saw a bat flying three o'clock high right in front of us. I yelled, "Hit the floor!" They all fell to the floor. I started crawling to the bathroom. They followed me on their hands and knees. Marvin took my white Eskimo coat, draped its hood over his head, and started swinging a broom at the bat. We peeked out the bathroom door and there was Marvin, swatting at the creature with my Eskimo coat swinging on his back.

The next morning another bat came flying through our bedroom. I screamed; this scared Marvin so badly that he jumped out of bed and hit his head on the light. By this time, we had a little white toy poodle named Pepper. Marvin threw Pepper out of his dog bed and used the bed to hit the bat. The bat flew into the back room. Marvin grabbed the door to close it, but because of his extra adrenaline, he pulled the door off its hinges. The door fell down on his bare feet and tore off his toenails.

Eventually the day for our first anniversary arrived. Somehow we both had survived that first year. We were happy and excited. It was a beautiful day, and Marvin was cooking steaks out on the grill on the back porch. I was preparing baked potatoes, salads, and things. The anticipation was too much for me, however. I broke out in hives all over my body. Marvin had to call his mother, and she came over and bathed me in Epsom salt. To make us feel better, she got out our wedding cake top we had saved in the freezer, but it had gotten freezer burn and turned to sawdust. Neither one of us will ever forget our first year of marriage or our first anniversary.

Chapter 11
Married Life

Not forsaking the assembling of ourselves together.

Hebrews 10:25

At the very beginning of our marriage, we traveled every Sunday to Grace Baptist Church in Anderson. But as North Manchester was a two-hour drive one way, it became too far to drive every Sunday. So we withdrew our membership and looked for a good church in North Manchester. We attended different churches here and there but never really got situated in any one church. Life settled into a normal routine of college and work. I still read my Bible and prayed, but without a shepherd to lead us, nor fellowship with other believers, we fell away from our closeness to God. I still loved God, but my love had grown cold. I had lost my first love. "Thou hast left thy first love" (Revelation 2:4).

Three years passed, and I graduated from Manchester College with a bachelor of science degree in elementary education in 1971. Marvin and I were both twenty-two years old. I submitted my application for a teaching position in North Manchester and the surrounding areas, but I never was hired. So, I put my applications out farther. I was hired as the kindergarten teacher at Maconaquah School Corporation in Bunker Hill, Indiana.

However, at this point in our marriage we made a grave mistake. We followed my teaching position, thinking it would bring in more money, instead of following Marvin's job and the promised position as plant foreman. We accepted my teaching position and left Marvin's position behind, moving to Peru, Indiana.

We sold our house to Marvin's grandfather, Samuel Blocher, for five thousand dollars, which paid off the remainder of my college loan. Because Mother was so poor, my first year at Ball State University had been completely paid for by a government grant, but when I was married and transferred to Manchester College, the cost was ten thousand dollars for the remaining three years, resulting in the loan.

We rented a trailer in a trailer park in Peru, and all seemed well. I was making nine thousand dollars a year, which was a lot of money back then. Marvin got a job at Globe Industries making modular homes. He worked his way up to plant purchasing agent. Things were good for about a year, and then Globe Industries closed their doors, putting Marvin out of a job.

However, he soon found another job as line foreman at the Eck-Adams factory. We moved out of the trailer park and rented a real nice small, two-bedroom home at 31 McKinley Avenue in Peru for $195 a month. My teaching position was going well. While I was teaching I continued my education, completing my master's degree at Ball State University. I became the head kindergarten teacher and supervisor over four kindergarten teachers in other schools. We were making more money than ever before. Finally, we bought a lot in a new housing subdivision in Peru and built a new home on Orchard Lane. We had two Doberman pinscher dogs, Nikia and Hyde, and owned two new vehicles free and clear. Life was good.

Answered Prayer

We started attending the First Baptist Church in Peru, but we were never faithful attendees. I would tell myself that I was going to start being more faithful to church, start reading my Bible faithfully every day, and have a stronger prayer life. While I would start, it would last for only a few months, and then the cares of this world would crowd in and I would slack off again. It was a never-ending spiritual battle.

Because we didn't truly have a home church and fellowship with other believers, I had no support group, no encouragement, and no spiritual guidance. Marvin was too busy with work and was gone a lot because he had taken a second part-time job. Through the week he worked his normal job at the Eck-Adams factory as line foreman, but he also started working with a construction company that operated out of town on the weekends. He was away from home a lot, and it was during this time I noticed that he seemed more distant. But I just overlooked it.

By this point we had been married for eight years and yet had no children. My constant prayer was, "Lord, if you would bless us with children, we would raise them in a church and be faithful." God heard my heart's desire and answered my prayer.

In February 1976, our brother-in-law, Ed Bunsold, offered Marvin a job as manager of his grocery store, Bunsold's Super Valu in Winchester, Indiana. Marvin accepted the position and we rented a two-story home at 421 Thompson Street, Winchester. It was then that I found out I was pregnant with our first child, Joshua. Ed told Marvin that he had several job requirements. One of these requirements was that we attend a church in the community, be faithful, and be of good standing in the community.

Wasn't that a strange job requirement? But it wasn't Ed—it was God. God was answering my heart's deepest prayer, to raise our children in a church, by making us accountable.

Chapter 12

A Church Family

How good and how pleasant it is for brethren to dwell together in unity!

Psalm 133:1

We moved to Winchester, and Marvin started working at Ed's grocery store, Bunsold's Super Valu. I had accumulated a lot of paid leave days at the school, so I took an early leave and quit in February 1976, because I was pregnant and it was too far to drive from Winchester to Peru. It was fun staying home, and I totally enjoyed being pregnant. I hardly ever felt sick.

We started attending Main Street Christian Church in Winchester, with Reverend Richard Merriman as our pastor. This was the same church that my sister, Margie, and her husband, Ed, attended. It was a very warm and friendly church, and the church members took us right into their church family. Margie, in particular, was very welcoming to me. For the first time since Daddy had died, I felt at home in a church. I'm the type of person who needs one close friend who I can feel safe around. When I had been with Linda, I didn't have that insecure feeling, but she now was married to Charles Abernathy and they lived in North

Carolina. The Lord knew I needed one close friend to bring me out of my insecurity.

Margie became that close friend. She encouraged me to get involved with ladies' groups and Coffee Friendship Bible studies. Margie and I had such a delightful time. Every week she and I would go to a Bible study in the home of a different lady. The most wonderful thing was that most of the ladies in the Bible study were also pregnant. Margie was pregnant with her third child, Marcus. She already had Tasha and Jeffrey, who were seven and four years old at the time. Two other ladies in the group, Nina Coe and Kathie Fields, were also pregnant. Isn't God wonderful to have given me Christian fellowship and bonding with other ladies right at the time I needed it most? God had answered my heart-felt prayer.

What a wonderful time we all had studying God's Word together, praying together, and crying together. We were all very emotional at this time because we were all so very pregnant.

I grew leaps and bounds in my Christian faith and felt loved and accepted by all. It was during one of these Bible studies, while I was sitting on the porch at Nina Coe's home, that it became very clear to me that I wasn't sinning outwardly, such as stealing, killing, or committing adultery; my sins were inward sins of my attitude, my motives, and my thoughts.

This new understanding impacted me greatly. I started having personal devotions and prayer every morning. I drew closer and closer to God. I started memorizing Scripture and meditating on God's Word. I praised Him daily for the precious little life developing inside me. I was twenty-eight years old, and I just loved being pregnant. I will always remember it as the best time of my life.

On December 16, 1976, our first son, Joshua Mark, was born. "Children are an heritage of the Lord: and the fruit of the womb is his reward" (Psalm 127:3). Joshua was a true gift from God—and how we loved him and welcomed him into our lives. From the first Sunday that Joshua was brought home from the hospital, he was in the church nursery, and on December 24, when he was nine days old, Joshua was Baby Jesus in the church Christmas pageant.

Soon after Joshua was born, we bought a nice, large, four-bedroom home on 403 South High Street, Winchester. Two and half years later, on June 6, 1979, God blessed us with another child, our second son, Isaac Michael. He was another precious gift from God and truly lived up to his name, which means laughter. He was such a happy baby and always laughing. Isaac also played as Baby Jesus in the church Christmas pageant, although he was six months old. So we now had two little souls to teach and train up in the Lord. God had answered my deepest heart-felt prayer of raising my children in a church to be faithful.

When a couple has a child, they begin to see life differently. Priorities change, and they feel responsible for that little soul they brought into this world. It is overwhelming just knowing that you are responsible for the safety and well-being of this new little life. Somehow you feel accountable to God. These little lives given to us are really only borrowed from God for a short time, and God expects us to teach and nurture them in the ways of the Lord. "Bring them up in the nurture and admonition of the Lord" (Ephesians 6:4).

Joshua

Isaac

Answered Prayer

When I was pregnant with Joshua, and we still lived at 421 Thompson Street, Margie gave me a book called *My Heart— Christ's Home*, by Robert Boyd Munger. It really touched my heart and gave me a new insight about my devotional time. Munger talked about how when we are saved, Christ comes to live in our heart. He describes our heart as a home having rooms: a library, dining room, drawing room, workshop, rumpus room, and that hall closet. He talked about how Jesus wanted to be Lord and master of all these rooms, including the tightly locked secret hall closet. As I read about each room, I began to search my own heart, I asked God to cleanse each room, one by one, and make them fit for His Holy Spirit to abide there. The book talked about how God wants absolute surrender and complete obedience. It described how Jesus wants to meet with us early every morning and spend time together. This is a special time for Jesus, too, the book says, because He longs for our fellowship.

The living room grabbed my heart the most. In the living room, there was a fire in the fireplace and Jesus was sitting in a chair next to the fireplace waiting for me. Also there was an empty chair for me.

Munger said to pick a special spot in a room, and a special time; and every morning Jesus will come and wait quietly and patiently to have fellowship with me.

Our home on Thompson Street had a small upstairs bedroom, which was going to be the nursery. It was wallpapered with bright yellow and orange flowers and had orange variegated carpet. It had two large windows, one on either side of a corner of the room. I placed a wooden rocking chair between the two windows. In the morning, that chair looked so warm and inviting when the sun rose in the east and shined bright colors through the window that reflected on the wall. The morning sunlight filled that small room with what seemed to be God's own presence. I made a covenant with Jesus to meet Him there early every morning at sunrise and start our day together.

I met with Jesus every day, and we grew closer and closer. However, once Joshua was born, some days I felt too busy with him to take time for my devotions. Then one day, as I passed by the room and the sunlight was shining through the window reflecting beautiful colors on the wall, it seemed I saw Jesus sitting there waiting patiently for me. It broke my heart to think He was sitting there alone, waiting for me. I walked into the room, knelt down at the chair, and asked Jesus to forgive me for leaving Him alone and breaking my covenant I made with Him.

From that time on, I started to be faithful in meeting with Jesus every morning in our special room. What a joy and peace we shared together. The song "In the Garden" took on a whole new meaning. It was as if I could smell the roses. Jesus made my heart sing when He revealed to me His truths and hidden mysteries.

No longer do I need a close friend to feel safe and secure; now Jesus is my closest friend and my constant companion. "There is a friend that sticketh closer than a brother" (Proverbs 18:24). This became a time in my spiritual growth that allowed me to catch a small glimpse of God's holiness. God works on us like little onions, peeling off one layer at a time, ever so thin. With each layer, He removes wrong thoughts, wrong attitudes, and wrong motives. He is at all times, ever so gently, conforming us to His image. I was growing closer to God day by day. To this very day, I still meet with my best friend early every morning, and we start our day together.

The Blocher family, 1980

Chapter 13

My Darkest Days

*If we confess our sins, he is faithful
and just to forgive us our sins.*

1 John 1:9

Marvin and I reached the point where we had been married for eleven years. As time had passed, I had reveled in the love I'd found in Jesus—raising my family and immersing myself in my daily devotions. By this time it was 1979, and we'd spent the previous three years in Winchester. We were members of Main Street Christian Church pastored by the Reverend Richard Merriam, whom Marvin and I grew to love. For much of that time, life was good, but I gradually had become aware that there was something seriously wrong in our marriage. Marvin had grown more distant. He also began to drink, and little by little, he descended into the darkness of alcoholism. I mourned the loss of the man I once knew.

During the most recent two years in Winchester, I had been called upon to endure the darkest days of my life. I'm not going into details on the happenings of this time, because God tells us not to give an evil report. All I will say is that our marriage was falling apart. Marvin had become a victim to alcohol. He still went to work every day, and there was no alcohol in the house, but on the weekends he would go to the bars and not come home till the early morning hours. Nothing destroys a family more than alcohol. Because of all this, I was contemplating leaving him. I had told no one about our problem, not even Margie. Therefore, I had no one to go to for consolation but Jesus, and I cried out to Him from the depths of my soul.

One morning after Marvin came home about 6:00 a.m. from being out all night, he and I were sitting at the kitchen table. Joshua was two and one-half years old and Isaac was one year old. I had just recovered from a miscarriage a few months earlier. It was our third child; I had been at four months of pregnancy. We never knew if the child was a boy or a girl, but I always believed in my heart that it was a boy, and his name would have been Isaiah. While sitting at the table, I told Marvin that I was not going to raise our sons this way and I was leaving him. He just sat there in silence, looking down at the table.

At that moment someone knocked at the door. It was Randy, a good friend of ours. He had come over to invite us to visit his church that evening for revival meetings. He was carrying a Bible in his hand. I couldn't believe it, but Marvin told him that we would come. (Many months later, Marvin told me that when he saw this friend at the door, he knew he was an angel sent by God.)

If God lays it upon your heart to do something, do it immediately. Who knows what decisions wait in the balance? If this friend had delayed in heeding God's call and the prompting of the Holy Spirit to come to our home at that very moment, I most likely would have already been gone when he arrived. The Holy Spirit directs and moves our spirit to do something, but it is up to us to obey.

Answered Prayer

We went to the revival meeting that night at a little Baptist country church. During the invitation, Marvin went forward and wept bitterly at the altar. I had never seen him cry that hard before. Several of the churchmen came up, put their arms around him, and prayed with him. We went home, and I decided to stay and work things out.

A few days later, after Marvin had asked God's forgiveness for his drinking, the Lord laid it upon his heart that he had to make things right with me and ask for my forgiveness. As Oswald Chambers wrote in *My Utmost for His Highest*: "When the Holy Spirit arouses a man's conscience unto repentance, it is the beginning of understanding God, and it brings him to the very threshold of God's presence. True conviction and true repentance brings a man to only one conclusion. 'Against thee, and thee only, have I sinned.'" Marvin seemed to be in much turmoil, and in the early part of the evening he left the house. At that time, I didn't know where he went, but later I found out that he went into some woods behind an old mansion on a nearby street and prayed, asking for God to direct him and intercede. He pleaded with God to give him the strength and courage to ask for my forgiveness. He was gone for hours walking and crying out to God. I knew something was desperately wrong, but I didn't know what. I called Ed, my brother-in-law, and asked him to pray for Marvin. I told him that I didn't know where Marvin was but that I could tell he was in great distress.

While in the woods, Marvin asked God to promise him that if he told me the truth—including other personal failings beyond the drinking—God would work all things out between him and me and our marriage would be okay; otherwise, Marvin would keep the truth hidden the rest of his life and go to his grave taking all secrets with him.

That night God gave Marvin that promise, and a sense of peace and tranquility came over him. He knew he could trust God's promise to work all this out for good. If we obey God's Word, and do what is right no matter how hard the thing is, God will work things together for our good. Marvin claimed the verse that says, "All things work together for good to those that love the Lord and are called according to his purpose" (Romans 8:28).

"God's conviction, forgiveness, and holiness are so intertwined that only the forgiven man experiences true peace" (Oswald Chambers). As the publican in Luke 18:9-14 prayed "God be merciful unto me a sinner," so did Marvin pray, and both the publican and Marvin went down to their house justified.

Marvin came home and confessed everything to me. It all had started in Peru when he was working with that construction company and was gone on the weekends. I had realized back then that he had started drinking and was becoming more distant. Marvin confessed that besides the drinking, he had been unfaithful to me. He said, "I've repented and asked Jesus to forgive me, and now I'm asking you to forgive me." He added, "God told me that I had to tell you and make it right."

"Wow!" I thought. Now I had the problem. I had to forgive. I guess I had had my suspicions, but my love had made me blind. I immediately said, "I forgive you," but down deep in my heart, like Jonah of old, who pouted that God had forgiven Nineveh, I pouted that God had forgiven Marvin so easily and completely. It didn't seem fair, and I felt betrayed. I never even considered the agony Jesus had already suffered for that forgiveness, which I thought had been so easy. In reality, it cost Jesus the heart-wrenching agony of the cross.

As days went on, I became lost in my own grief. I sat for hours in a dark room, alone. It's odd how if you give Satan a crack, he will rush in and flood your heart and mind with darkness.

In those dark hours, Satan was filling me with self-pity. Satan got ahold of my mind in a way he never had gotten ahold of me before. Isn't that just like Satan to rob any light Jesus has put in and cloak it with Satan's darkness?

This went on for days, and I progressed into deep depression. It was as though Satan had me in his jaws of despair. Marvin didn't know what to do. Here he had done the right thing—done what God told him to do—and yet everything was falling apart. Marvin cried out to God and reminded Him of His promise that He would work these things out if Marvin told me and made things right with me.

One day Marvin came home from work and found me in such a deep state of depression that he came over, put his arms around me, and called out to God to bind up Satan. I, too, knew I had to get ahold of myself before Satan completely engulfed my mind. I whispered, "God help me." I continued whispering as Marvin prayed to bind up Satan. And God, in His infinite mercy, reached down and touched me.

I started talking to Marvin again, which I hadn't done in days. We prayed together and asked God to heal my mind. I knew that the center of my problem was unforgiveness. I asked God to give me a forgiving heart and the love to forget. Amy Carmichael wrote about this: "If I say, 'Yes, I forgive, but I cannot forget', then I know nothing of Calvary love."

I knew that if forgiveness was to come, and for my mind to be completely healed, I needed to study God's Word. I got out the books we had from the Bill Gothard seminar and began to study the section on forgiveness. I started memorizing Scripture and meditating on God's Word, for I knew that the Word of God has cleansing power.

I pleaded for the blood of Jesus Christ to cleanse my heart and mind, and God started purging my thoughts and mind. I could feel His cleansing power flowing through me.

I studied the parable in Matthew 18:23-35. It tells about a certain king who took account of what his servants owed him. One servant was brought before him that owed him a great amount. The king demanded payment, but the servant could not pay his debt. The king ordered that the servant be sold in order to repay his debt. The servant fell to his knees and begged for mercy from his lord. The king was moved with compassion and released him, forgiving him all his debt. Then, that same servant went out and found one of his fellow servants who owed him only a small amount. He took him by the throat and said, "Pay me what you owe." His fellow servant fell to his knees and begged for mercy. But he would not show mercy, and he cast his fellow servant into prison till he paid his debt. The king found out about this and said, "You wicked servant, I forgave you of much, and you cannot forgive a little. Then neither shall I forgive you." And the king cast the servant into prison till he paid all his debt.

It was then I realized that if I did not forgive Marvin, God would not forgive me. I fell to my knees and asked God to forgive me and take away my unforgiving spirit. It was not in me, but by God's grace I forgave and I was set free. "If the Son therefore shall make you free, ye shall be free indeed" (John 8:36).

Sin is sin. God does not see one sin greater than another. He sees them all the same, and Christ had to die on the cross for all our sins, whether great or small. No sin is small to God, because they all cost the wrenching agony of our Savior.

So often, until we've gone through some deep valley of hurt, heartache, or betrayal, our Christian faith is shallow. We've never been called upon to test our faith or prove God's faithfulness. If you've ever been crushed deeply, you understand what I'm saying. Call upon the all-knowing and all-caring God. He loves you and knows exactly how you feel.

Answered Prayer

There is no knife that cuts deeper than betrayal. But remember, Christ also was betrayed. It is through these times of soul searching that we grow in Christ. We never know why God allows us to go through these trials; however, we will understand perfectly once we get to heaven. Then, all things will be revealed to us of God's amazing design for our lives. But until then, we simply must trust Him. Perhaps the purpose is to help and encourage others who are going through the same trials. Until you've been there, you can't help others. Hurting people don't want to listen to someone who hasn't felt the same pain they are suffering. We are to be witnesses of God's all-sufficient grace and that He is able to deliver us.

As I look back on this dark time in my life, I thank Jesus for giving me the strength to come through it as a much stronger person, drawn closer to my Lord. God is faithful and able to heal our broken hearts, and that's what He did for me. I realized that there was a specific purpose, a reason, why I was born. I realized that simply leaving the man I'd come to love was not the right thing to do. But before God would bring His plan into focus in my life, He wanted my absolute surrender, my unreserved obedience, and my total abandonment of all else but God.

Chapter 14

Renewal

> What therefore God hath joined together, let no man put asunder.
>
> Mark 10:9

Marvin and I were both changed. We had a new love for each other and a new commitment to each other and to God. Marvin was a new creature in Christ, and he never drank again. Second Corinthians 5:17 became my verse for our marriage: "Therefore if any man be in Christ, he is a new creature: old things are passed away; behold all things are become new." My soul could bear witness to the renewal of the Holy Spirit within Marvin. (Today, as I write this, we just celebrated our forty-fifth anniversary. People so often ask us, "How did you last so long? What is the secret?" Christ is the secret. Every marriage will go through hard times at one time or another. But Jesus is the healer. Jesus is the answer.)

We attended the advanced Bill Gothard seminar, and we both just seemed to soak in God's principles. After the seminar, we decided that it would be to our advantage to get rid of the television set. It was a brand new solid state, so we donated it to

Winchester High School. We replaced it with a new stereo sound system, and I filled our home with Christian music.

On our thirteenth wedding anniversary, September 22, 1981, we decided to go back and visit Grace Baptist Church in Anderson, where we had been married and where Pastor Don Camp was still the pastor. It just so happened that on that Sunday, they were showing a movie called *Thief in the Night,* and in the evening they were going to show its sequel, *Distant Thunder.* We were so impressed with the morning service that we went back for the evening service. It was like a new awakening to us. We started driving every Sunday to Anderson, an hour drive one way. For several months we attended Grace Baptist Church.

Finally, we scheduled a meeting with Pastor Don Camp and told him all that had transpired in our marriage for the past thirteen years. After listening, he told us that he felt that God was calling us out of Winchester. He said, "I see it as a spiritual move." We put our house up for sale and started looking for houses in Anderson. Herman Landus was the realtor showing us around in Anderson.

God directed our every step. Marvin had always wanted to be a dairy farmer like his parents. I had never lived on a farm, but I was willing to learn. Joshua was five years old and Isaac was three. Grace Baptist Church had a school connected with it, called Indiana Christian Academy, and we both felt it would be good for the children to go to a Christian school. (However, I ended up homeschooling the boys.) In 1981, we withdrew our membership at Main Street Christian Church and joined Grace Baptist Church in Anderson.

Then the Lord started opening doors. Herman Landus owned a fifty-acre farm in Anderson. Late one night he called us and asked if we would be interested in renting the farm for two hundred dollars a month. Then he said that the last renter left it an absolute mess and that if we cleaned it up, mowed the yard, and took care of his farm, called Merry Woods, which was right next to the farm that we would be renting, our rent would be free for the first year. We said, "Yes, that would be great." I sat on the bed and cried tears of joy. I praised God all night. What an answer to prayer.

It was a big undertaking. In August 1981, Marvin left Ed's employment at Bunsold's Super Valu. Marvin was so happy and felt like this was his dream come true. Our house in Winchester sold. We went to a farm auction in Berne, Indiana, and bought milking equipment, a tractor, baler, manure spreader, hay conditioner, and everything else we would need to start a dairy farm. With the money from the house, we paid off our farm equipment, and with the extra money we bought twenty-five head of Jersey dairy cows. God also provided twenty acres of bottomland for hay. It had not been cut for four years, and the owner said that if we baled it, the hay would be free. This was another answer to prayer.

The Blocher family, 1981

Chapter 15

The Farm House

The Lord directeth our steps.

Proverbs 16:9

The farm we rented had a large two-hundred-year-old farmhouse built in the 1700s, and there was a big old barn that was built at the same time with hewn beams and pegs. It was a scary old house. It was believed that the basement had a secret passageway, which had been closed off, that led to the barn and had been used to transport slaves in the Underground Railroad. The secret passageway was connected to an old fireplace in the basement. The opening of the fireplace had since been shut with concrete. The boys found the trap door in the barn where users of the passageway would have emerged. It was a very intriguing old house, but there was only one problem: it was haunted.

The first night that we stayed in the house, there was thunder and lightning with strong winds blowing. A tree branch was rubbing against the house, making an eerie growling and scratching sound. Our four-wheel-drive truck got stuck in the front yard when there really was no reason for it to get stuck. It was on a flat place and the ground was not even muddy. But all the truck would do was slide back and forth. It was as if something or someone was holding it back. I had to go out and help Marvin try to get it unstuck, so that left the children alone in the house. They were frightened and bawling their eyes out. Then the lights went out. The tree branch was scraping louder against the side of the house and screeching. The lightning was cracking loud with thunderbolts. The boys were in the dark, and I had no flashlight. It was a very scary night that never seemed to end, and it was not a good beginning in our new house.

The truck never did get unstuck that night. In the morning, we had to have the next-door farmer pull it with his tractor.

That first night we slept there I had a dream. I dreamed I saw a cross burning in the front yard and I knew in my dream that it was started by the Ku Klux Klan. There was screaming and hollering, and then I woke up. I was very frightened and I wondered what type of house had we moved into. On the day after we moved in, I went to the library and looked up the history of this old house. It didn't mention the Underground Railroad, but I found out that a little girl had fallen down the stairs in the living room and died. The strange thing was that even before I found this out, every time I walked up the staircase in the living room, I would have shivers running down my back. Also, at night the music box would start playing when no one had touched it. Yes, the house was haunted.

I closed off the front part of the house by hanging sheets over the doorways. The front part of the house included a large living room with an antique chandelier and beautiful hardwood floors, four large windows stretched from the ceiling to the floor. In its day, it would have been very elegant, but now it seemed to hold a cold, eerie feeling. There was a staircase on one side of the living room, and the other side of the living room led into a wake room, where prior residents had shown the bodies of people who died.

Answered Prayer

In the old days, they did not use funeral homes; they kept the bodies in the house. The staircase led up to a landing with three large bedrooms. I never went into the front part of the house, and I played Christian music all day long in order to take away the cold, eerie feeling.

It was a large old farmhouse. The front part of the house was the original farmhouse. The part we lived in had been added on sometime later. It included a small living room, a formal dining room that had a large ornate antique walnut table with chairs, a large old kitchen with a trap door in the floor leading to the basement, another room off from the kitchen, one bathroom, and two bedrooms.

Once our church had the Maranatha Singers for an evening concert, and we volunteered to house two boys from the group for the night. I always thought it was important for our boys to be around other young men who were serving the Lord. It just so happened that that night, after we got the boys home, it started storming very badly with lightning and thunder. Then the lights went out, of course. Not only did that make the house scary, but it also meant that we had no water, because we were on a well and we had to have electricity for the well pump to work. The only place in which I had room for them to sleep was on cots in the haunted front living room. I did not tell our guests it was haunted. Because the lights were out, we had to use candles. I was carrying a three-tiered candelabra, leading the two boys into the haunted living room to show them were they were going to sleep. The storm was getting worse, and there was more lightning and thunder. Shadows from the trees blowing in the wind came through those tall windows and cast scary, dancing images on the walls. I felt like I was in a scary movie leading them into "dark shadows."

Somehow, our guests survived the night. In the morning I asked them how they had slept. Eric said, "It was the eeriest, coldest night I've ever spent in a house, and I kept hearing strange noises all night long." In the morning, the electricity was still out, so we had to milk the cows by hand. Eric came down to the barn to help us milk the cows. He had been raised on a farm and knew how to milk a cow.

The other boy was the piano player for the Maranatha Singers, and he said, "I can't take the chance of hurting my fingers." So he stayed in the house with our boys.

When it was time for them to leave, Eric said, "Wow, this was quite adventurous, and I'll never forget it." I never did tell them that the house was haunted.

MR. AND MRS. BLOCHAR, JIM, JOSHUA, ISAAC,
   THANK YOU VERY MUCH FOR HAVING US
IN YOUR HOME. THE FOOD, FELLOWSHIP, AND
FARMING WAS GREAT. IT WAS GOOD TO GET
UNDER THE UDDER AGAIN! THANK YOU FOR
THE BOOKS ALSO — WE APPRECIATE GOOD
READING MATERIAL. MAY THE LORD BLESS
YOU AS YOU DO HIS WILL HERE IN ANDERSON.
THANKS AGAIN!
                        IN CHRIST,
                        Eric Barnes
                              Prov 20:6
                        David Anderson
                              II Tim. 2:15

Maranatha Singers—Eric is the tall one

There was another incident that occurred later, just a few months before we moved from that house. Early one morning, while it was still dark out, Marvin had already gone down to the barn, and the boys and I were still in bed asleep. Suddenly something hit the house with such a great force that the windows shook and it seemed as if an evil presence entered the house. I'm not sure what it was, but I would say it was a demon. It scared Joshua so badly that he crawled under his bed to hide. Isaac remained asleep. My body was literally immobilized in my bed. I was lying face down, and it felt as if someone was pushing my face into the pillow, trying to suffocate me. I could not move or speak. I perceived that it was an evil spirit. Out of the side of my mouth, which was all I could move, I muttered, "Jesus, Jesus, Jesus." That released me enough that I was able to sit up in the bed. I sat up and yelled, "In the name of Jesus Christ I rebuke you and demand you to leave this house." Suddenly, all was calm.

That was a scary experience for all of us. Joshua said, "I will never forget it." And neither will I.

We lived there for two years, and physically, it was the hardest two years of my life. I remember being in the hayloft of the barn listening to the cold wind blowing through the cracks of the wooden-beam walls with such an eerie whistle that I just threw myself up against the wall and cried, "Oh God, help us through this winter." Both boys were too small to help us with any of the work. Joshua drove the tractor and Bobcat every now and then, but Marvin and I did all the physical work and heavy lifting.

We milked our twenty-five head of Jersey cows twice a day—once at three o'clock in the morning and again at three in the afternoon. While they were being milked, we fed them grain. We kept our grain in a large metal grain bin. Once when I went to get the grain, the bin was low on grain, so I had to bend down far into it to reach the grain. I kept feeling a puff of wind blowing across my face. I went and told Marvin that something was blowing air on my face in the grain bin. He brought a flashlight and looked into the bin. There were two large rats. They had been jumping at my face. Marvin got the shotgun from the house and shot them.

We baled 3,500 bales of hay. I drove the tractor while Marvin put the bales on the wagon. Then it was up to us alone to put the hay up in the hayloft. We planted twenty-seven acres of soybeans and sixteen acres of wheat. It was an all-day, every-day operation. We both aged ten years in those two years.

But it was also a wonderful time. We grew in the Lord and renewed our love for each other. One warm night, after the boys were asleep, we took a blanket out and lay on the ground looking up at the stars. I had never seen so many stars before in my life, and they just seemed to twinkle. It was a beautiful night and all was peaceful with only the sound of the locusts making their chirping sounds. There was the smell of lilacs in the air. It seemed like a magical night. Marvin reached over and put his hand on mine, and my heart was full of love and joy in my marriage and in Jesus.

The boys loved the farm. We named all twenty-five of our Jersey cows—these are the cows with big beautiful brown eyes—and we loved them dearly. We had twelve baby calves that we had to bottle feed, and of course we named them all. Our other animals included two pigs, named Piggle and Wiggle (the first time I heard them eat, I said, "My goodness, they eat like pigs!"); one Black Angus beef cow, named Babe; one baby bull, named Brother Don after our pastor; one young Jersey cow, with a club foot, named Angel, which we all loved and babied; two Doberman pinschers, named Nikia and Bykota; one stray dog, called Rags;

and of course, lots of cats. There was the large old barn the boys could romp around in, and acres and acres to run and play in. I homeschooled Joshua, so both boys were always home. Life was good.

Then suddenly things started to happen. Our cows and calves started to die. Our two pigs died—one baked to death and the other froze to death. Our milk production decreased to a point so low that we could hardly survive. We became as poor as church mice. We ate oatmeal three times a day, because that was all we could afford. We churned our own butter; it was the boys' job to shake the jar of cream. We made our own jam and canned our own vegetables from our garden. Marvin kept the garden free of weeds.

Even with all these hardships, we still stayed strong in our love for each other and tried to make things fun for the boys. As a family, we would go pick wild raspberries together, and then I would make the jam, which everyone loved. At Christmas, we were so poor that the boys only got one ten-dollar toy each. They both got red trucks. But they didn't know we were poor. To them we were happy, and they just loved being together as a family.

The church could see that things were not going well for us. At Christmas, the church usually helped one family. We were the family the church decided to help with food and money. The day they came out to visit, we had a sick baby calf, named Rosebud, lying on the kitchen floor, which we were bottle feeding. They gave us food and money and prayed with us. We all prayed that Rosebud would live, which she did. Finally, things at our farm became so bad that I sold my wedding ring and bought a Jersey cow. I named her Diamond. But she died too. (Later on we found out that we were feeding the cows moldy hay, and that was why they were aborting their calves and even dying themselves.)

Answered Prayer

To continue our cleanup of the farm, Marvin took the truck and went out trimming the vegetation along the fence rows, accompanied by Joshua, who was five years old. But while Marvin was cutting, the chain saw jumped back and cut his left knee to the bone. Joshua steered the truck home, while Marvin had his foot on the gas pedal. Thank God Marvin didn't lose his leg. It took twenty-two stitches on the inside to hold the muscle and tissue and fourteen stitches on the outside. He was laid up for a while, but I couldn't keep him down. He still came out to the barn and helped me milk.

Things had to change. We could no longer survive on the farm. After Marvin healed up, he took a job working for Ron Halbert at the Bus Mart. I went around looking for a house to rent, because Herman Landus had sold the farm and we had to get out. Every place I went had just been rented right before I got there. Things seemed hopeless.

There was a house at 3100 West Cross Street that Marvin kept telling me to go check into. It was for sale. I knew we didn't have money for a down payment, so I never would go. Finally I obeyed my husband and went to speak to the people who owned the home. It was owned by Mr. and Mrs. Dilts. They were excited that we were interested in buying it. Apparently, God had stopped anyone else from even looking at it.

The Cross Street property turned out to be a five-acre farm. I told them we didn't have any money, but they said they would sell it to us on contract for forty-five thousand dollars, at 9 percent interest, with three thousand dollars down. What an answer to prayer.

We sold our hay conditioner to come up with the down payment. We sold the rest of the equipment at Mort Shirley's Auction in order to pay off a loan we had taken out to buy improved equipment for the farming. Then we sold our cows back to the people we had bought them from.

To get some of the equipment to the auction, I had to drive the tractor that pulled the manure spreader some twenty miles down a major highway. It was a dreary fall day with a light mist, and I was very cold. It was a difficult drive for me because of all the traffic and I had to pull off the road several times. I had to wait for several hours for Marvin to get to the auction site, because he was still at the farm hooking up more equipment to bring to the auction. When I finally got there, I was so exhausted that I crawled into the back of the manure spreader, curled up, and fell asleep. However, the Lord worked all this out, and the five-acre farm God allowed us to buy was a true answer to prayer.

On the dairy farm—Joshua, age 5, and Isaac, age 3

Chapter 16

The Five-Acre Farm

A blessing, if ye obey . . .

Deuteronomy 11:27

In 1984, we moved into the five-acre farm God had provided. Would you believe that the day we moved in was the first day Marvin ever saw the house? He was too busy with the farm equipment to come and see it with me earlier. He said, "If you like it, that will be good enough for me." What a trusting soul. The night we moved in, we had a pastor come with us who went from room to room and prayed over each room, blessing them so no evil spirit could follow us from that old farmhouse. Believe me—I was glad to be out of that haunted house. Joshua was seven years old and Isaac was five, and we all loved our new home. It had three bedrooms, one bathroom, a living room, a dining room that I called the kitchen nook, a nice-sized kitchen, a utility room, and a two-car attached garage. It was perfect for us.

Marvin purchased a barn shown in an ad in *Farm Weekly*. The barn was twenty-eight by forty-eight feet. It was already torn down and we just had to reconstruct it. Marion, Marvin's brother, came over and helped him build the barn.

We loved the house, but we soon found out why no one ever looked at it. It was built on a swamp. Every time it rained, we flooded, and the bottom part of our house, which included the utility room and garage, was a foot or more under water. Our entire house would be surrounded by water, but it never came up into the part of the house that we lived in. Once, the water was so deep that Joshua literally stepped out of the back door, got into the canoe, and rowed to the barn. The main part of our house was up high, and—thank God—the water remained in the downstairs part of the house in the large utility room and garage. This water problem never altered our faith in God's provision. God is good, and this was the house He had provided for us. We were happy in it and just trusted Him to give us the strength to endure.

When it didn't rain, our backyard was beautiful. Our backyard was at least a half an acre. It had Indiana pine trees, large maple trees, fruit trees, lilac trees, and redbud trees. Our fruit trees included apple, peach, pear, plum, and cherry trees. Marvin put a swing out in the middle of the large maple tree area, and I would go out there early in the morning, sit on the swing, and have my devotions. Listening to the breeze whistling through the pine trees and feeling it blow through my hair made me feel peaceful and close to God. I would sit there, open my hymnal, sing songs of praise, and read my Bible. How I loved the house God had given me.

Once the boys were a little older, we bought an Allis-Chalmers tractor with a bucket. Our five-acre farm was long and narrow with a hill in the middle. This hill was the problem, because it kept the water from draining into the county ditch that was down the field on the other side of the hill. With the tractor and bucket, Marvin and the boys dug a 1,300-foot-long ditch all the way down the field and through the hill. It helped with our flooding but never totally eliminated it.

Answered Prayer

Marvin was always a hard worker. On top of working at the Bus Mart as a mechanic, he also drove motor coaches for Econoway Motor Coach, which was also owned by Ron Halbert. He had a chartered trip going to Wyoming, and we, as a family, were allowed to go with him. It was a Nazarene church group from Plymouth, Michigan. We had such a wonderful time on the bus. It's the first time the boys heard praise songs such as "Our God Is an Awesome God." They both loved it, and it was a good Christian experience.

When we got to Wyoming, it was a whole new adventure for the boys. We went on horse rides and mountain climbs, and we even camped out on the prairie. One of the camp directors came up to us and told us that our oldest son, Joshua, was a natural-born horse rider. I'd never heard of such a thing. But I did know that Joshua could control his horse better than anyone there, especially me. Every time I went on a horse ride, my horse would end up on the top of the hill, while all the other horses and their riders were on the trail at the bottom of the hill. I would be yelling and screaming all the way. Everybody would say, "What are you doing up there?" I'd say, "I don't know, the horse just went up here on his own." I had no control of my horse at all, but it was a wonderful trip with good Christian people and was something the boys will never forget.

Marvin worked hard and would do whatever it took to support his family. I didn't work, so he was the sole provider. In order to do this, he took on additional jobs. Not only did he work at the Bus Mart and drive motor coaches, but he also got a job helping a farmer bale his hay.

They baled the hay and took it to a doctor's farm for his horses. The doctor was Dr. Paul Jarrett. When Marvin was done putting the hay in the barn, he told Dr. Jarrett about our boys and that I homeschooled them. Marvin asked if it would be okay to bring them down sometime to ride horses. Dr. Jarrett said, "Yes, that would be fine. You can bring them down right now, if you like."

Marvin came straight home and told me, and we immediately took the boys to Dr. Jarrett's horse farm. He had nineteen horses. He told the boys, "Since you are homeschooled, you could came down every day and help clean stalls and comb the horses. I will teach you how to ride." Then he said, "And I'll even pay you a little something for your work." The boys were thrilled. What an answer to prayer.

I had been praying that the Lord would provide something for the boys to do other than just riding their bikes. We still did not have a TV—which I am so glad about, because not having a TV allowed the boys to become very creative. Ever since the Wyoming trip, they had both loved horses. I made a commitment to bring the boys down to Dr. Jarrett's every day. I considered this to be their physical education class.

The name we gave to our home school was Christian Life Academy. Each day started with Bible reading and prayer. Then the boys both practiced their piano. They took piano lessons once a week with Mrs. Boley. Dr. Jarrett taught them how to ride English Flat Saddle. We had a good home school experience, and the boys were learning a lot and doing well in their studies.

Dr. Jarrett liked the boys and said that he had two Morgan horses he would sell us—Valentine and Lance. Valentine had been Mid-America Champion at the age of three. She was now seven years old. Lance was not a champion horse, but he was very well trained. We already had the barn, so we bought the horses. The boys were nine and seven years old at this time. When Joshua turned ten, he joined the Mane and Tail 4-H Club. Soon Isaac also was old enough to join.

Both boys saw great success in 4-H with their horses. Our house was full of trophies and ribbons, which I proudly displayed. Joshua especially excelled in his horse riding and won championships in almost every class he entered. Dr. Jarrett could see that Joshua had exceptional talent in horse riding, so he also taught him how to drive a two-wheeled cart and entered him in the pleasure-driving classes in competitions. Joshua and Valentine won every pleasure driving class they entered, even at the Indiana State Fair.

Because of Dr. Jarrett's encouragement, we joined the Morgan Horse Association and the Ethan Allen Morgan Youth Club. Joshua won trophy after trophy. At one of the Morgan Horse Association shows, Dr. Jarrett entered Joshua in a National Pleasure Driving class against World and National Champion horses and drivers. There were about twenty contestants in the class. Joshua won third place. He became the top winner in the Morgan Horse Association for three years in a row. They put his name on their large perpetual silver cup trophy, meaning it shall remain there forever. He was in the newspaper so much that he became a celebrity. He truly was a natural born horse rider.

Not only did both boys show their horses, but they also showed their dogs. Joshua showed his English setter, named Applejack, and Isaac showed his Brittany spaniel, named Brittany. They won Grand Champion and Reserve Grand Champion in the 4-H dog show. They also were in 4-H shooting sports and learned how to shoot their pellet guns. Both boys also joined the YMCA and took judo classes. We were busy. Without doubt, the boys had an adventurous life, and the five-acre farm was a blessing from God and a true answer to prayer.

Isaac and Joshua in their English riding suits

*Isaac with Brittany—
Grand Champion*

*Joshua with Applejack—First
Place in Showmanship*

Joshua, age 10, with 4-H trophies and Morgan Association trophies

Joshua—Pleasure Driving—Grand Champion

*Isaac and Lance—
English Flat Saddle*

*Joshua and Valentine—
English Flat Saddle*

Answered Prayer

The boys loved the farm and their horses. Homeschooling gave them freedom that most kids didn't have. They went to the middle of the field and built a log cabin out of old lumber. They had everything they needed—dishes, iron skillets, blankets, and lots of candles and matches.

They would take their horses into the field and camp out. Once, Marcus, their cousin, came over to camp out with them. I gave them a whole chicken from the freezer to take down and cook on the fire pit. It was dark, and the only light the three boys had was from the fire. They all were famished, and it seemed like the chicken was taking forever to cook. They became tired of waiting and decided to just eat the chicken. They said to each other, "That is the best tasting chicken I've ever eaten." Then they went to sleep in their cabin. When the morning came, they looked at the chicken bones and saw they were uncooked. They had eaten the chicken raw.

One day Marvin brought home a little Honda 65 dirt bike from the shop. Joshua tied a rope behind it, attached a tire to the rope, and pulled Isaac around the field. Joshua drove around and around. Isaac had on a pair of Chinese-looking goggles and was holding on to the tire for dear life, laughing all the way. When Joshua stopped, Isaac was completely covered with black dirt. When Isaac took off his goggles, all you could see were two white circles around his eyes and white teeth. The boys just loved it.

When Joshua was ten years old, he built a tack room in the barn, all by himself. Then he got out his dad's electrical books and wired the entire barn, without help. Marvin looked it over and said that he couldn't have done it any better himself. Marvin also taught the boys welding, soldering, and woodworking. I considered this to be their vocational school. The wiring that Joshua installed is still being used in that barn to this very day.

Both the boys learned to work hard. There was always work to be done on the farm, such as cleaning stalls, feeding and watering the horses, trimming the horses' hooves (which Joshua learned), mowing the back field, baling hay, and putting hay up in the hayloft.

They also learned things that other kids would never have time to learn. I wanted to instill a love for reading in the boys. I gave them free time to just sit around and read. They both learned to love to read. Isaac loved science books, geology books, and mystery books such as *The Hardy Boys* and *Sherlock Holmes*. Isaac even started writing a mystery story himself. Joshua liked pioneer books such as *Little House on the Prairie*. Then Joshua became interested in survival books. He learned how to find edible plants and survive in the wilderness.

He learned how to tan hides, which he did often. He'd go down the field, shoot a rabbit, come home, and tan its hide. I had a special freezer downstairs that was full of Joshua's hides. We had three calf hides that were given to him by his Uncle Don. There were three deer hides, a sheep hide, four deer feet, and one deer head, which Joshua was going to use to learn how to do taxidermy. That freezer achieved a bit of fame the time Aunt Marlene came to visit. We were cooking dinner and I needed an additional ingredient. Aunt Marlene said she'd get it. I heard her scream a few minutes later: "Oh, my goodness! A deer head!" The boys went running, and I followed. Aunt Marlene was standing in front of the freezer, her arm outstretched, her right index finger aimed at the deer head. I had always been afraid someone would look into that freezer. It was a scary sight.

It wasn't unusual to see Joshua come back from a nearby wood carrying a log on his shoulder. From that log he would hand carve a bow and make his own arrows. We took the boys to the historic Mississinewa Battlefield where they reenacted the War of 1812 along the Mississinewa River. People would come from all around, dress up according to the period, and camp out along the Mississinewa River for three days. They had the French and Indian War reenactment, Indian villages, wilderness camps with trappers and mountain men, traditional crafts, music, songs, and stories of the time. Both boys loved to dress up when we went to the War of 1812 Mississinewa battlefield. We bought Joshua leather and hides so he could make his own mountain man outfit complete with knee-high moccasins and a full-bodied fox skin hat. Isaac liked the rabbit furs. He wore an old leather jacket with leather fringe, a raccoon hat, and moccasins. It was always the highlight of our family fall trips. We also went to Civil War reenactments. We bought Joshua a rifle kit so he could make his own 40-caliber Thompson black powder rifle. Joshua was quite the outdoorsman.

Isaac was a gentler sort. He loved space, stars, and crystals. We bought him a professional telescope so he could study the stars and moon. In his bedroom we put up a huge mural of the planets and outer space. We took him to gem shows. He also loved *Star Trek*, so we took him to the Indianapolis Convention Center for a *Star Trek* convention. He loved it. His bedroom was full of beautiful crystals, gems, and *Star Trek* collections.

I could tell that he had a good voice and loved to sing, so I enrolled him in voice lessons at Anderson University with a professional voice teacher. He did exceptionally well, and she said, "Isaac has a lot of natural talent and a beautiful singing voice." We continued singing lessons all the way through his high school years.

Isaac also loved cameras and taking pictures. He would take pictures of everyone and everything with his flashcube camera. Once he took his camera and flashed my face so much that I grabbed his camera and chased him down. I was going to flash it in his face, but accidently I had the camera turned the wrong way and flashed it at my own face. I saw spots for hours.

Isaac became interested in the television and movie industry. We took him to a PBS event at Ball State University during one of their telethons. They allowed him to run the TV cameras. He also wanted to be on TV commercials. I took him to Indianapolis and enrolled him with a talent agent. They took headshots and did photo shoots. I even made him an entire outfit to look like Jim Carrey's in *The Truman Show*, right down to the suitcase. Isaac looked identical to the Truman character and was a smash hit.

A couple times, Isaac was called upon to do auditions for TV commercial advertisements. For one of the auditions, we bought him a new tan-colored pair of shorts, a golf shirt, and a tennis racket. He was to stand there like a model in a magazine. They almost selected him, but then they chose someone else. Isaac also was invited to go to the Heartland Film Festival in Indianapolis. He had on his tuxedo and looked so handsome. They took his picture with Maureen O'Hara as well as with John Dye from the TV series *Touched by an Angel*.

Isaac always seemed to be in the fast lane going somewhere and thinking of new and different ways to do things. He had quite the entrepreneur mind.

The boys and I were together around the clock, and we were busy with all their events. We went everywhere together and did everything together. We called ourselves the Three Musketeers. I never took them somewhere and just dropped them off; I always stayed and watched them do whatever event or class they were in. They didn't mind having their mother with them, like some other kids did. Homeschooling removed all peer pressure. They didn't care what other kids thought; they cared what we thought.

Homeschooling allowed me to teach them godly family values and instill godly character. It kept them from worldly influences. Deuteronomy 6:7 tells us, "Thou shalt teach them [God's commandments and statues] diligently unto thy children, and shalt talk of them when thou sittest in thine house, and when thou walkest by the way, and when thou liest down, and when thou risest up." That is exactly what I was trying to do. You can't just tell them these things; they have to see them in practice.

Godly values and godly character cannot be taught; they must be "caught." They are learned little by little as we walk together and talk, as we sit together and talk, and as we pray together before our children lie down to sleep. It is a lifestyle they must hear, see, and learn, as I experienced with Lucille.

Both boys accepted Jesus Christ as their personal Savior at a young age, which spared them a lot of heartache. I continued to homeschool both boys all the way through their elementary and high school years.

Homeschooling was life to me. I was not just homeschooling; I was planting godly seed so that when the time was ripe for it to come forth, it would produce righteousness. Each day I would start my personal devotions with this prayer: "Lord, here are my two sons, may they grow to love and serve you." God had answered my deepest prayer that we would be able to raise our children in a godly home and be involved in a good church.

The Blocher family, 1997

Joshua's senior picture, 1995

Isaac's senior picture, 1998

Joshua's high school graduation, 1995

Isaac's high school graduation, 1998

Chapter 17

Growing in Grace

Grow in grace, and in the knowledge of our Lord and Saviour Jesus Christ.

2 Peter 3:18

Life on our little farm remained good for the next decade or more. The years passed, the boys progressed into their teenage years, and Marvin and I were in our forties. As a family, we grew in our devotion to the Lord. We worked hard, as always, and we rejoiced in the fellowship we enjoyed at church. Even though I was busy with the boys and homeschooling, I still had my personal devotions every morning without fail at 5:00 a.m. before I got the boys up. Marvin and I always got up at 4:00. I made his lunch, and after he left for work, I had my devotional time.

We were involved in Grace Baptist Church and growing in the Lord. Pastor Don Camp, who had pastored the church for twenty-five years, resigned in 1984, because he was diagnosed with Parkinson's disease. (He died fifteen years later but was bedridden for ten of those years.) Pastor Leigh Crockett took his place. Pastor Crockett also was a dynamic preacher, and we grew to love him. Our whole family grew spiritually under his preaching. I thank God for Grace Baptist Church. For ten years it rooted and grounded our boys in the Lord and enriched our marriage.

Yet physical hardship visited us in 1994. I was forced to have a hysterectomy; this related back to a miscarriage I had suffered earlier on the dairy farm in 1982. When we first moved to the dairy farm, I had a second miscarriage. I was only three months along. This is what happened: Marvin had gone down into the basement of the farmhouse. The entrance to the basement was through a trap door in the floor of the kitchen, and it was extremely heavy. He was trying to hook up a weighted pulley so we could lift the door more easily. While he was down in the basement, the chain snapped, dropping the entire weight of the door on Marvin's back. He yelled, "Help!" I grabbed the rope and pulled the door off his back, but it strained my belly. From that time on, I started to bleed, and a few days later I had my second miscarriage. This caused me female problems from that time on, so in April of 1994, I had a hysterectomy.

Marvin's mother came over and took care of me. She was a great help. She loved to listen to Christian music, so we played it the whole time she was there. She died two months later on June 2, 1994 from a heart attack. I was so glad I was able to spend that special time with her. Marvin's dad had died one year earlier on February 11, 1993 from cancer. My mother had died seven years before that on September 25, 1987, also from cancer. Her husband, Lawrence, had passed away a few years earlier. After his death, Mother moved to Bremerton, Washington. Walter also moved to Bremerton and had married Maureen. Margie and I went out to Washington to visit them the year before Mother died. We never returned for her funeral. Margie and I wanted to remember Mother the way she was the last time we saw her.

After my hysterectomy, I had to gain my strength back, so Isaac and I started walking at Shadyside Park. We walked every morning in sunshine, rain, cold, and even snow. It was our time to walk and talk together as Deuteronomy 6:7 tells us to. It was a time for me to instill godly character in him. By the time one year had passed, I had regained my former strength plus some. I had lost sixty-five pounds. It was 1995, and Joshua had graduated from our home school, Christian Life Academy. He had been accepted at Vincennes University in Vincennes, Indiana, and had gone off to college. Isaac was still home. It was his senior year.

In our devotional time, which Isaac and I still had every morning, I wanted to talk about Christian people who the Lord had brought through trials, so I got out Bill Gothard's books called *Heroes of the Faith*. They consisted of six different books about these persons: Susanna Wesley, who was the mother of Charles and John Wesley; Adoniram Judson, who was the first missionary to Burma in the 1700s; John Newton, a slave trader who became saved and wrote the hymn "Amazing Grace"; Gladys Aylward, who led one hundred children across the Shensi Mountains to safety from the Communist Red China Army; Dwight L. Moody, an American who was the greatest preacher of England in the 1800s; and Oswald Chambers, who wrote *My Utmost for His Highest*.

I chose the book on Oswald Chambers simply because it had pictures of Egyptian pyramids and camels. I didn't like fictional books, but I loved reading true stories about people whom God brought through hardships. As I started reading the life of Oswald Chambers, who lived from 1874 to 1917, God touched my heart deeply. It was as if God reached down and gave my soul a new awakening. I saw my wretchedness before a holy and righteous God. I sat on the couch for three days crying, confessing my sins, and asking God to forgive me and to give me a new heart, a heart totally devoted to Him. Isaac would see me crying and could see that I was under deep conviction, but he did not see the transformation that was happening inside. He would say, "I'm going to take that book away from you." (What's funny is, I can go back and read that same book today and not be affected in the way I was then. It was the Holy Spirit working in my heart at that particular time in my life.)

Somehow I was changed. I started writing a diary for the first time in my life at the age of forty-six. I never used to like to write before. I never even wrote letters. Suddenly, I was writing and writing. Also, I couldn't get enough of the Word. I started reading the entire Bible and memorizing Scripture, which seemed to come easier. Marvin bought me the dramatized audio King James Version of the Bible on CD by Alexander Scourby. I started writing daily devotionals and started writing poems. Previously I had never even liked poetry. I remember the first time I wrote a poem, which was unintentional. It was this: "Thank you Jesus for food to eat, for dishes to wash, for floors to sweep. Thank you Jesus for a lovely home to keep." I wrote beside it, "I think I wrote a poem!"

Soon poems were flowing through my mind like water. Daily devotionals were coming faster than I could write them down. My prayer life increased to hours, and I literally prayed without ceasing. I was changed. There was a renewing of my mind.

One evening while I was sitting on the couch, which is where I always sat and wrote, Isaac came out of his bedroom and pointed his finger at me. "Thus says the Lord," he said. "Write these devotionals down in a book."

I looked at him and said, "Okay, Prophet Isaac." It seemed funny at the time, but I started doing just that. I entitled it "Diary of the Heart." It started out being a separate diary in which I wrote just my poems.

Every day God would give me a new poem or a new devotional thought. I would write the devotional thoughts in my regular diary that I wrote in every day, but I would put a star (*) beside it in order to distinguish it from my everyday entries. Then I wrote my corresponding poem for that devotional in the second diary. I was able to correlate each devotional and corresponding poem by the recorded date of when I had written them. I planned to use these devotionals someday, each as a one-day reading, whenever I was able to complete my "Diary of the Heart." My childhood prayer, that I would daily have devotions and draw closer to God, had come true.

In 1998, Isaac graduated from our home school, Christian Life Academy, and was accepted at Bob Jones University in South Carolina. Joshua had since graduated from Vincennes University with an associate's degree in conservation law enforcement, and was currently attending Indiana University to study law enforcement and park management. When Isaac left for Bob Jones University in 1998, I got the dreaded empty-nest syndrome.

It was hard on me not to have my children around me. They were my life and now they were gone, totally. As long as Isaac was home, even though Joshua was gone and in college, I was okay. Now, with the last bird out of the nest, I felt empty. One night I was moping around the house, unable to sleep, so at 2:00 a.m., Marvin took me to Wal-Mart, because they were open twenty-four hours. He told me to buy something in hopes to make me happy again. I bought sheets in order to make new curtains for our bedroom. It did give me something to do and make me happy. I enjoyed sewing and redecorating our bedroom. I made sheets, curtains, pillowcases, a bed skirt, and matching pillows for the top of the bed. I even drew a matching picture to hang on the wall.

Joshua graduated from Indiana University in 1999 with a bachelor of science degree in law enforcement and park management. He married Nancy Hall on August 7, 1999, and they now have two children, Hunter and Hope.

In 1999, Isaac transferred from Bob Jones University to Anderson University, during which time he lived at home, which I totally enjoyed. He graduated in 2001 from Anderson University with a bachelor of arts degree in communications and film production. Then he moved out to California, where he got a job with Phil Cooke Pictures, where he did his internship.

Graduation from Indiana University, 1999

Officer Joshua Blocher— Noblesville Police, 2000

Joshua—Indiana University Police, 1999

Isaac—Graduation from Anderson University, 2001

Isaac, 2010

Isaac in Los Angeles, 2003

With both boys gone, Marvin and I were alone, again. Here's a poem I wrote about it:

Isn't Life Funny?

Life is so often filled with stages.
You first get married
And try to learn how to live with your husband.
Then the children come along.
At first it's great,
Then you start to feel trapped,
As a mother at home with wee-small babies.
You can't go anywhere,
Because you can't afford a babysitter,
And you don't really want to get one anyway.
All you have going for you are diapers and bottles.
I remember some days looking at the babies and saying,
"What have I done? I've ruined my life!"
But as time goes on,
You get used to their little voices
And life as a mom.
Soon your children become your life.
You forget what life was like without them,
And you love them more than life itself.
As they grow older, they become your best friend.
You become their chauffeur.
It seems all you get done is
Dropping them off and picking them up.
Then the great day comes when they get their license.
You think, "Finally, some rest!"
But instead, you find out you've lost them.
Once they get their wheels they are—gone.

Answered Prayer

Now, instead of entertaining them,
You are praying for them,
Because they are doing—who knows what?
Then they get married.
You think it's great,
Until the shock hits you
That you won't be seeing them every day,
Or even once a week.
You miss them terribly.
You can't imagine life without them.
Then, all of a sudden
There is your husband,
Who you have to learn to live with
All over again!
Isn't life funny?

Marvin and Josie, 2003

Chapter 18

Following His Lead

Follow after the things which make for peace.

Romans 14:19

Within a couple years after the boys were gone, it became apparent that keeping up with all the farm work and the horses was too much for Marvin. We both were fifty-three years old. Marvin's health was starting to go downhill. He was diagnosed with arterial vascular disease and had to have leg bypass surgery. At the same time, they thought he had Crohn's disease, but instead it turned out to be irritable bowel syndrome (IBS). At any rate, we had to sell the farm and move to a condominium, where someone else would take care of the mowing and the outside of the building.

We called Dennis Jackson Auction Barn, put the farm up for auction, scheduled an auction date for five weeks later, and started looking at condominiums. At the time, Marvin owned his own school bus and was a private school bus driver for Yorktown Schools, plus he still worked at the Bus Mart. I had just been hired at Yorktown Schools as a bus driver. So he was thinking it would be better for us to move to Muncie.

Marvin found a condominium he liked in Muncie. We had been living in Anderson for twenty-two years—two years on the dairy farm and twenty years at the house God had given us—and I sure didn't want to move to Muncie, but Marvin said, "Let's go look at this condo in Muncie."

I fought the idea and said, "There's no way I'm going to move to Muncie." My stubborn, disobedient self was showing its ugly face again. Marvin, again, had more foresight than I did.

That night I could not sleep, which is very unusual for me. I usually slept like a baby as soon as my head hit the pillow. But not that night; my spirit was troubled. I went out to the couch and sat there, and it seemed as if the Lord said to my mind, "Josephine, when will you learn to obey your husband?"

I fell to my knees and said, "Yes, Lord, forgive me. I will obey my husband."

When the morning came and Marvin got up, I said, "If you still want to go look at that condo—okay, I'll go." He got dressed right then and wanted to leave immediately. It was for sale by the owner. When we got there, Marvin walked right up to the door and knocked. A woman came to the door. He said, "We're interested in looking at your house." The people who owned it were Mr. and Mrs. Timmons. They were happy to show us through.

When I first walked in the door and saw how beautiful it was, I said to myself, "Oh my, there's no way we can afford this." Marvin fell in love with it immediately.

They were asking $125,000. In my mind that was more than we could afford. But Marvin told them that we would go talk about it and get right back with them. It was still early in the morning, so we went and got coffee and donuts and drove to a nearby park. Marvin wanted to write an offer for $122,000 including all appliances and the entire bedroom with matching bathroom décor. In about an hour, we went back and gave them our written offer. They accepted it.

Now, everything had to be put into motion. The farm auction was set for August 25, 2003. I had to pack all the kitchen things I would be keeping, along with all my knick-knacks, books, and clothes, and get everything ready for the auction. We had once again accumulated a lot of equipment—both farm equipment and horse equipment. All equipment had to be sold. We gave Valentine and Lance to a friend who had young children and loved horses. We knew the horses would have a good home and that we could see them anytime we wanted.

The condominium we were moving into only had one bedroom, so we had to downsize. It was overwhelming.

On the day of the auction, Margie and some of our church ladies came over and helped me set out on tables all the things I had decided to put in the auction. It covered the entire horse arena, which was about forty-five by eighty-five feet. We had borrowed twenty-five long rectangle tables from the church. They were completely covered, and the entire arena was packed full. Marvin couldn't believe I had so much, but I know how to stash a lot of stuff. I went a little hog-wild in selling everything; it was as if I had thought I was going to die. I sold our bed and bedroom suite, the boys' beds and dresser, two kitchen tables and chairs with a buffet, our living room set from downstairs, my complete strawberry set of dishes (which was a mistake), dish after dish, and pan after pan.

Marvin, too, went hog-wild in putting things in the auction. He sold rakes, hoes, shovels, and lawn mowers. We sold the horse cart and horse tack and all horse equipment we hadn't already given to the people who took Valentine and Lance. We had another tractor to sell, a plow, a disc, and an old farm truck. It was a big auction.

When the selling commenced, I was a nervous wreck. They sold all the small stuff first, and then they sold the farm. They started the bid for the farm at $105,000. No one was bidding. Then finally, this old man held up his hand. The farm sold for $105,000. We had three days to decide whether we were going to accept the bid. At first, we were going to pass and not sell it, because we were hoping for $140,000. That night was a sad one. We had no furniture, not even a bed.

We did have one couch and love seat I kept, but other than that the house seemed empty. We both just walked through the house feeling sad, not knowing what the future held. This had been our home for twenty years. The boys grew up here, and it held our memories.

Then Joshua came over and brought us a large blow-up bed. He said, "I know you didn't get what you wanted for the farm, but you need to accept the bid and sell the farm because of Dad's health." Joshua could tell we were down in the dumps, so he stayed a while and kept us company.

Because of Joshua coming over that night and encouraging us, we did accept the bid. At the closing, the old man who bought it said, "I didn't want to buy the farm. I just raised my hand in order to start the bidding. But since no one else bid, I guess I bought the farm." Then he said, "In my days when a man made a bid on something, he made it good, so I will." He paid cash. Praise God, the Lord sold the farm when no one came to buy it. The old man died six months later.

Once the sale closed, we had $105,000 plus $5,000 from all the other things that we sold at the auction. Several years earlier we had paid off the $45,000 farm contract. However, we got an equity line and remodeled, so now we owed the bank some money. But the amount we got for the farm was enough to pay off the bank, put a sizeable amount down on the condominium, buy all-new furniture, and still have money in the bank. The Lord is good.

We moved into our condominium on September 3, 2003. A new chapter in our life was about to begin.

Chapter 19

Starting Anew

Delight thyself also in the Lord; and he
shall give thee the desires of thine heart.

Psalm 37:14

Our condominium was not new, but it was like new to us. It had been built in 1998 and was only five years old. We loved it. It had a brick gas-log fireplace in the living room and a nice-sized kitchen with lots of oak cabinets in just the color I liked. The best things about the condominium were that it had a very large family room and a large bathroom with a Jacuzzi. It also had a second bathroom connected to our bedroom. It had only one bedroom, but that was perfect for us. It was the most beautiful home I'd ever seen. I had bought new sheets for our new bed, and the first night we slept there, they felt so crisp and clean that I said, "I feel like we're in some rich person's house and in the morning we'll have to leave."

Marvin said, "I feel the same way."

Never in all our married life had we such a beautiful home, and we thanked God for it.

Marvin still worked at the Bus Mart and drove a school bus for Yorktown Schools. I was a new bus driver. Everything was new for me. I had a new home, new job, and new town, but I didn't want to start at a new church. Grace Baptist Church in Anderson was where we had been married thirty-five years earlier, and we wanted to keep our roots there. But upon moving to Muncie, instead of being only ten minutes away, we were thirty minutes away. We stayed at our church, however, and made the drive every Sunday.

Things were good. Marvin's health was improving. He went to work every day at the Bus Mart and Yorktown Schools. I drove the bus every day whether there was sunshine, rain, snow, or ice. Marvin and I got up each workday at 4:00 a.m. I made his lunch, and he left for work at 5:00 a.m. From that time until 6:00 a.m. I had my own personal devotional time of reading the Bible and prayer, and then I wrote my own poems and devotionals. I hated having to quit at six o'clock and get ready to go drive the school bus. It seemed like the flow of my thoughts was always interrupted. On the way to the school, I would listen to my Bible CDs. When I got to the school I would start my bus, in order to warm it up, and then go sit in my car. During those fifteen minutes, I would write down some devotional thoughts that had come to mind while driving to school. My mind was in constant thought about what I wanted to write.

By this time, I had completed a four-month devotional collection. It was one big book containing 120 single-day devotionals together with their correlating poems. I had Staples bind it in a spiral binder. However, I still needed to complete eight more months' worth of devotionals (245 of them) in order to have a complete 365-day collection for a one-year devotional. I knew I already had that many devotional entries written in my diaries that I had starred; however, by now I had written forty-one diaries and seven poem diaries. In order to find my devotionals, I would have to read through all my diaries together with my correlating poem diaries. This all took time, which I didn't have. The morning hours were when God gave most of my poems and devotional thoughts to me. I say they were given by God because there was no way I could have written these devotionals and poems on my own. They were a gift from God—He gives, I gather.

After the school bus route was over around eight o'clock in the morning, the day became busy with life. I was also a realtor, first with Re/Max and later with F. C. Tucker/Five Star, so I had to be at the office for a time, too. It seemed that around 1:00 p.m. I would have time to start writing again, but I had to quit at 2:00 p.m. and leave and go drive the bus route. I was in a constant struggle trying to find time to write down all the thoughts that were flowing through my mind. This went on for four years.

Then in 2007, Marvin fell off a twenty-foot ladder while working at the Bus Mart. He landed on concrete and crushed his left heel. Dr. Brokaw at Ortho Indy told him that this was a life-changing accident. He said that Marvin would never walk correctly again and that he would be in constant pain.

Dr. Brokaw was right. It took a year for Marvin to heal, and he has never been the same after that. He has permanent nerve damage and is always in pain.

Marvin couldn't do all the hard work at the Bus Mart anymore, so he quit. He found he could no longer count on his school bus driving job either, since at the time all contracts for private school bus drivers were expiring and the school was not going to renew them. But by God's grace, Yorktown Schools hired him as their full-time mechanic.

Also, by this time, since I was a realtor, we had bought fifteen rental properties. So not only did I drive the school bus and work at the realty office, but also I managed our fifteen properties, plus I managed the properties of five other people. I was a busy lady. The struggle continued to find time to write my devotionals and poems, which was my heart's desire.

Chapter 20

Tragedy

Trust in the Lord with all thine heart; and lean not unto thy own understanding.

Proverbs 3:5

In autumn 2010, Marvin and I were both 61 years old. Marvin had been the Yorktown Schools bus mechanic for two years, and I was in my seventh year of driving a school bus. On the morning of September 15, it was a bright and sunny day, and I had just finished driving the morning route and had parked my bus. Marvin came over to talk to me, and we were both standing in front of my bus. I had just turned to walk to my car when a high school student, driving a light green Volkswagen, came flying into the parking lot. She was late to school and talking on her cell phone. She apparently didn't see me and she hit me at about 30 miles per hour. The back of my head broke her windshield. I slid down the front of the car with the breath knocked out of me, and then I went unconscious. When she slammed on the brakes I was launched fifteen feet into the air. I landed twenty feet away on the asphalt like a rag doll. Marvin thought I was dead. She just missed hitting Marvin, who had been standing next me.

When I regained consciousness, I could not move. The EMTs were called. Once they arrived they said, "Josie can you feel this?" I said, "Feel what?" My legs were paralyzed for a short time. They put me on a hard, flat board and tied down my head, arms, and legs. In the ambulance the EMT said, "You are lucky to be alive."

While being transported to the hospital, the question came to my mind, "Why did this happen?" Then the answer echoed through my mind: "That Christ be gloried through it." I believe that nothing can happen to a Christian unless it is first sifted through the loving hands of our Lord. All things He allows are for a greater purpose, and Jesus will give us the strength to endure whatever trial he calls upon us to face.

Once X-rays were taken, they determined that I had two fractures in my pelvic bone (on my left side in front and back); a fractured sternum; a fractured clavicle; several fractured ribs; and a badly bruised left shoulder and elbow. My right leg was swollen to three times its normal size. My head was bleeding from crashing against the windshield. I had a concussion, and my right ear had benign postural vertigo, which made me feel like I was spinning.

I was in the intensive care unit for five days. I was administered morphine every two hours. I could not move, turn over, or sit up. I had to be turned by a sheet. I was in extreme pain. I felt like Jonah when he said, "I cried by reason of mine affliction unto the Lord, and he heard me. Thou hast cast me into the deep, in the midst of the sea; the floods compassed me about; all thy billows and waves passed over me. I went down to the bottoms of the mountains; the earth with her bars was about me. When my soul fainted within me I remembered the Lord, and my prayers came up unto thee" (Jonah 2:2-7). And God comforted me.

Marvin stayed with me the whole time. Isaac flew in from California. Joshua and Nancy came to the hospital. Churches began to pray, and God heard.

The days in the ICU were extremely hard, but God gave me the strength to endure and gave me a verse to cling to. "Bow down thine ear, O Lord, hear me: for I am poor and needy. Save thy servant that trusteth in thee" (Psalm 86:1). This verse gave me strength. I could hardly speak, nor could I move, and I knew God would bow down his ear and hear the whispers of my heart.

Marvin stayed right by my side. My sister, Margie, came and stayed with me. Isaac, who was an EMT, said he would stay in the hospital room with me all night. They brought him a bed and he took care of me. Isaac stayed with me for five days in the ICU. They were going to keep me three more days in a regular hospital room, but because Isaac had EMT training and was going to stay in Indiana, they released me into his care.

On September 19, I left the hospital and went home. Marvin was going to take care of me, and Isaac was going to stay for two more weeks.

When I finally got home, I was helpless. I was in a wheelchair, and to go into the bathroom I had to use a walker, which was a major undertaking. I couldn't dress myself. I couldn't take a bath or wash my hair, which still had dried blood in it from when my head broke the windshield. I felt poor and needy. This is a poem I wrote:

Poor and Needy

Bow down thine ear, O Lord,
A whisper is all I can make.
Hear me, my Father,
For thy help, I beg.
I'm unable to do
For myself as I would.
My needs are more than I can bear.

> Poor and needy, poor and needy,
> This is my lot—despair.
> Hear me, Father, hear me,
> Thy strong arms I need.
> Hold me, Father, tightly,
> Sustain me. For I am weak.
> Carry me, Father, carry me,
> With manna feed.
> O Father, help me,
> I am poor and needy, indeed.
> Psalm 86:1

After two days, on September 21, the home care nurse came and started me on home care, physical therapy, and occupational therapy, where they teach you how to take care of yourself. I was in home care for six months. I had to go through repeated testing for my benign postural vertigo, which I called Chinese water torture. They took X-ray after X-ray of my pelvis. Finally, they told me that my pelvic bone was not healing. I had to wear a bone stimulator for a year. I developed tendonitis in my right ankle. It was a complete year before I was somewhat normal.

My life had changed. I couldn't come and go as I wanted to. I couldn't even sit and relax, because the break on my posterior pelvic bone was in the exact location where all the pressure is when a person sits. Even today, years later, I have to take a pillow with me everywhere. Marvin usually carries it for me. Isn't that sweet of him?

God used this time to draw me closer to Him and to direct my paths. It was a time of sitting still and worshipping at the feet of Jesus. There are no accidents with God. Not one single thing can happen without His permission. There is no circumstance that can prevent the will of God in your life. The will of God in every person's life is to lift up Christ no matter what circumstance or trial you are called upon to face and to draw closer to our Lord; and through our example, others will see Christ through us and draw closer to God. All through our lives, with every trial and hardship, God is faithful. He never leaves us desolate, but will always provide strength to endure. God's promise is, "I will never leave thee nor forsake thee" (Hebrews 13:5). God's allotted purpose in our life is to bring glory to Jesus Christ and for Him to teach us the way of holiness. God allows trials to exist in order to make us holy so we can come forth as gold. My prayer was that God's purpose for this accident be fulfilled. I believe it has been and still is.

The outpour of love and care was overwhelming. I had so many flowers, cards, meals, gifts, and people coming over to help that I needed to find a way to thank them all. The Lord impressed upon my mind to give a thirty-day devotional booklet to anyone who sent a letter, fixed a meal, visited, or helped in any way. Just the year before, I had assembled a thirty-day devotional entitled *Eternal Streams*. It consisted of some of the best devotionals and poems I had written several years earlier. The Lord laid it upon my heart to write my testimony about the accident on the inside cover. One hundred thirty copies of this devotional were sent out. My prayer was that it would touch the hearts of all who received it and draw them closer to God.

In earlier days, I had just wanted to be able to read, write about, and study God's Word without interruptions. I had lots of time now. There were no more interruptions to disturb the flow of my thoughts. During this time of healing, not only was God healing my body, but He was also teaching my mind and heart to trust Him. He filled me with His love and gave me a quiet peace to which nothing could compare.

I started compiling all my devotional writings. The Lord showed me that instead of making a one-year devotional collection of 365 entries, I could make twelve thirty-day devotional booklets. Each one would have its own title, such as *Eternal Streams, Desert Blooms*, etc., but all twelve would be part of a collection entitled "Diary of the Heart Series." I had never thought of this before. I started reading my old diaries and found page after page of devotionals that God had given me down through the years. The Lord also gave me new devotionals and poems. It seemed that I was writing a new poem or a new devotional every day.

Later, I looked in my diary to see what I had written one or two days before the accident. This is what I wrote on September 13, 2010:

> What does my life count for? When I'm dead and gone, will my short existence on earth have made any difference at all? I'm just a flower, a weed really, who flourishes for a moment, then the wind passes over it and it is gone, and the place thereof shall be remembered no more. Man is just a blade of grass, a leaf that withers, dew that melts, and a wind that blows. Each day seems long, and then all of a sudden sixty-one years have passed. Everything changes, nothing lasts, only God, only God. If only I could live a life that honored God, and made some small difference. A life worth remembering.

On April 12, 2011, seven months after my accident, the Lord took Lucille Zuercher home. Walter and Lucille had remained close to Marvin and me all the years of our marriage. They were part of our family. Walter Zuercher passed away ten years earlier on April 7, 2001. But Lucille's death especially was hard on me. I considered her my second mother and I loved her very much. She encouraged me in every endeavor I undertook, and I could truly feel the impact of her prayers. As Naomi was to Ruth in the Bible, Lucille was to me. The day I heard of her passing I was in the process of making her a Mother's Day poem book. She loved my poems and encouraged me to write. I felt a great loss that day. Lucille was my pillar, and God used her greatly to shape and mold my life. Her life was a godly testimony of God's faithfulness and love. She died on her birthday. She was eighty-eight years old. What a heavenly homecoming celebration that must have been.

Chapter 21

Reflections

For the Lord is good; his mercy is everlasting.

Psalm 100:5

One year after the accident, in August 2011, I returned to driving the school bus. It was harder to drive because the break on my posterior pelvic bone had formed scar tissue around it, which made it feel like I was constantly sitting on a stone. So I had to take my pillow everywhere. Marvin was still the Yorktown Schools bus mechanic, and I continued my realtor and property management activities. It seemed like that year just flew by compared to 2010, which was full of doctor visits and therapy. I continued writing my devotionals in the hopes of completing my twelve devotional booklets entitled "Diary of the Heart Series." During the summer of 2012, I finally completed all twelve of the thirty-day devotional booklets, thus making a full collection of 365 entries. I praised God for allowing me to finish it. It was my life's goal and ambition.

Here is a sample of the devotionals that God gave me. This is the first day's devotional in *Eternal Streams*:

Mystery of His Plan

"Having made known unto us the mystery of his will,
according to his good pleasure which
he hath purposed in himself."
Ephesians 1:9

Faithfulness through difficult times is what tries our mettle. It is easy to be faithful when everything is going well, but let things start falling apart and that's when we have to search our soul. Still, I have found that it's during these times of difficulty that I have grown closer to God. No, maybe I didn't see it at the time, but in retrospect I now realize it was during the trials, not the good times, that I grew in my Christian walk. With this in mind, one could ask the question—why does Christianity grow most in times of persecution? The answer is the same—in times like these we need a Savior.

Can God trust you with disappointments,
To put them in His hand?
Can God allow trials to press you,
Knowing you'll accept His plan?
Without prayers for removal,
Or the need to understand?
Only just to trust Him
In the mystery of His plan.

(The "Diary of the Heart Series" has not been published yet.)

Soon it was August 9, 2012, and it was time for school to resume. I returned to driving a school bus for the second year after the accident. This time, however, I was having a terrible time seeing the road on those dark mornings. Earlier that year I had been diagnosed with a ruptured optic nerve in the back of my left eye that required surgery. But that seemed to have healed and I thought all was well. I was fine driving the afternoon route because it was in daylight, but those dark mornings just looked black. I prayed every morning for God to give me protection and safety, and I drove slower than usual.

But soon everything seemed darker. I was turning on more lights in all places I went, and I was complaining about things being dark. I visited an eye specialist, and on October 10, 2012, I was diagnosed with severe glaucoma. I had already lost some sight in my left eye. Immediately I resigned from driving the school bus.

I praise God that before my eyesight reached this point of decline, He allowed me to complete all twelve of my thirty-day devotional booklets entitled "Diary of the Heart Series."

I have started to learn Braille on my own. Even if I don't need it now, it's better to learn it while I can still see than wait until I can't. My prayer is that if I do lose my eyesight, it will not be total blackness and at least I will be able to see light. But God is good. His mercies endure forever. I can trust Him to give me the grace to endure no matter what the future holds.

As I look down through history, there are many Christians who God allowed to endure physical ailments. Since I have glaucoma, which could possibly lead to blindness, the one in particular who comes to mind is Fanny Crosby. She lived from 1820 to 1915. She lost her eyesight at the age of six months when a quack doctor put hot mustard poultices on her eyes, leaving her blind. But she never felt resentful toward the man, believing it was allowed by God to fulfill His plan for her life. She was saved at the age of thirty-one while singing a song by Isaac Watts called

"Alas! And Did My Saviour Bleed?" Fanny Crosby became one of the most famous hymn writers of her time.

I, too, feel no resentment toward the girl who hit me, and I don't resent having glaucoma. God allowed both to fulfill His purpose for my life. I know I can trust Him and that He has only good planned for me. He never leaves His children hopeless. He is always there to encourage them, help them, and sustain them. I am learning more and more to trust Him along whatever path He leads me.

Oswald Chambers says, "When you are in the dark, listen, God is dealing with you. And if you listen, God will give you something you can share with others once you get into the light." When God takes us through darkness, we come out with God's light.

One of my father's favorite verses that gave him the strength to endure any trial he was called to face was Isaiah 41:10, and it shall also be my verse to see me through: "Fear thou not; for I am with thee: be not dismayed; for I am thy God: I will strengthen thee; yea, I will help thee; yea, I will uphold thee with the right hand of my righteousness."

Back in 1982, while living on the dairy farm, Marvin and I were having a Bible study in our home led by two of the deacons in our church. After the Bible study, we all talked about prayer. One of the deacons said, "I don't know how anyone can pray effectively without a prayer list." That night I started thinking about what he said. It was in that year that I started to make a prayer list. Because of that prayer list, I began recording my prayers and recording how they were answered. When a prayer was answered, I would write "Thank You, Jesus" beside it, jot a little note about how it was answered, and record the date. This is how this book got started, because I saw how there were so many answered prayers.

God always answers our prayers. But not always is His answer "yes." Sometimes His answer is "no" or "wait." It's like a child who asks his or her father for something, but because the father knows the danger of the world, or the future consequences of what the child asked for, his answer may be "no" or "wait."

Our heavenly Father loves to give good gifts to His children, but if our prayer is not answered the way we want, it is because God knows best. Amy Carmichael wrote about this in her booklet called *If*: "If when an answer I did not expect comes to a prayer which I believed I truly meant, I shrink back from it . . . and I fret inwardly and do not welcome His will, then I know nothing of Calvary love" (*If*, 69).

Sometimes we think our prayers are unanswered. Yet I know that there are no unanswered prayers. God answers them all. He just doesn't always send the answer we hoped for. When that happens, we have to accept God's will and let go of our own.

Oswald Chambers said, "We have to get into the habit of dealing with God about everything." Bring everything before the Lord and let Him deal with it. And remember, even no is an answer. Yet "the effectual fervent prayer of a righteous man availeth much" (James 5:16).

There is only one thing that will keep God from hearing our prayers, and that is sin. Psalm 66:18 says, "If I regard iniquity in my heart, the Lord will not hear me." I may pray, but if I am not rightly related to my heavenly Father, my prayers will not be heard. Oswald Chambers says, "Prayer is only effective when there is completeness." We first must be complete in Christ. That means we must be saved and rightly related to our heavenly Father. So often, we come frivolously before a holy and righteous God. Before we advance toward the throne of God to ask a petition, we first need to plead the blood of Jesus Christ upon our hearts. Then we proceed with a repentant heart, humbly bowing before our Lord and King.

God answers prayer—this we know. Yet as Oswald Chambers wrote, "We are not here to prove God answers prayer; we are here to be living monuments of God's grace."

We have come to the end of my story, for now. Lord willing, more shall follow. God has continued to bless and marvelously answer prayer. Marvin and I continue in our love and God gives us grace each day to continue. Joshua and Nancy and their children, Hunter and Hope, are a blessing to us and are growing in the Lord. Isaac, who has been in California for the past ten years, has been given a wonderful wife, Kristie Finch. They were married on April 6, 2013. The Lord has allowed us to pay off our home and be debt free. What a blessing! The Lord has given me more time to read and study God's Word and to write.

God has been extremely good, and His blessings are bountiful. My story may end for now, but God willing, it will continue, and my heart says with David:

Bless the Lord, O my soul:
And all that is within me,
Bless his holy name.
Bless the Lord, O my Soul,
And forget not all his benefits.
Who forgiveth all thine iniquities;
Who healeth all thy diseases;
Who redeemeth thy life from destruction;
Who crowneth thee with lovingkindness
And tender mercies;
Who satisfieth thy mouth with good things;
So that thy youth is renewed like the eagle's.
Bless the Lord O my soul."

Psalm 103:1-5

Marvin and Josie, 2007

Joshua, Nancy, and family, 2010

Hope and Hunter, 2011

Isaac and Kristie, 2013

Ed and Margie Bunsold

The Bunsold family—Ed, Margie, Tasha, Jeffrey, and Marcus

Margie, Walter, and Josie

Charles and Linda Abernathy

Linda and Josie

Josie and Linda

Josie Blocher

About the Author

Josie Blocher lives in Muncie, Indiana, with her husband, Marvin. They have been married forty-five years and have two sons, Joshua and Isaac. She has a bachelor of science degree and a master's degree in elementary education and currently helps run the family real estate business and manages their rental properties. Her love is writing devotionals and poetry. Several of her poems have been published by Warner Press and Famous Poets Press. She has written a yearly devotional series, yet to be published, entitled "Diary of the Heart." Also she has written and illustrated twenty children's books. Her heart's desire is to serve the Lord by honoring her husband and writing devotionals and poetry that touch and inspire hearts and reveal the faithfulness of God.